LOUIS ARMSTRONG'S HOT FIVE AND HOT SEVEN RECORDINGS

OXFORD STUDIES IN RECORDED JAZZ
Series Editor   JEREMY BARHAM

Louis Armstrong's Hot Five and Hot Seven Recordings
Brian Harker

The Studio Recordings of the Miles Davis Quintet, 1965–68
Keith Waters

LOUIS ARMSTRONG'S HOT FIVE AND HOT SEVEN RECORDINGS

BRIAN HARKER

OXFORD
UNIVERSITY PRESS

OXFORD
UNIVERSITY PRESS

Oxford University Press, Inc., publishes works that further
Oxford University's objective of excellence
in research, scholarship, and education.

Oxford   New York
Auckland   Cape Town   Dar es Salaam   Hong Kong   Karachi
Kuala Lumpur   Madrid   Melbourne   Mexico City   Nairobi
New Delhi   Shanghai   Taipei   Toronto

WITH OFFICES IN
Argentina   Austria   Brazil   Chile   Czech Republic   France   Greece
Guatemala   Hungary   Italy   Japan   Poland   Portugal   Singapore
South Korea   Switzerland   Thailand   Turkey   Ukraine   Vietnam

Copyright © 2011 by Oxford University Press, Inc.

Published by Oxford University Press, Inc.
198 Madison Avenue, New York, New York 10016

www.oup.com

Oxford is a registered trademark of Oxford University Press.

Library of Congress Cataloging-in-Publication Data
Harker, Brian.
Louis Armstrong's Hot Five and Hot Seven recordings / Brian Harker.
p. cm.—(Oxford studies in recorded jazz)
Includes bibliographical references and index.
ISBN 978-0-19-538841-1; 978-0-19-538840-4 (pbk.)
1. Armstrong, Louis, 1901–1971—Criticism and interpretation.
2. Jazz—1921–1930—History and criticism.
3. Hot Five—Discography.
4. Hot Seven—Discography. I. Title.
ML419.A75H37 2011
781.65092—dc22   2010019801

9 8 7 6 5 4 3 2

Printed in the United States of America on acid-free paper

SERIES PREFACE

THE OXFORD STUDIES IN Recorded Jazz series offers detailed historical, cultural, and technical analysis of jazz recordings across a broad spectrum of styles, periods, performing media, and nationalities. Each volume, authored by a leading scholar in the field, addresses either a single jazz album or a set of related recordings by one artist/group, placing the recordings fully in their historical and musical context, and thereby enriching our understanding of their cultural and creative significance.

With access to the latest scholarship and with an innovative and balanced approach to its subject matter, the series offers fresh perspectives on both well-known and neglected jazz repertoire. It sets out to renew musical debate in jazz scholarship, and to develop the subtle critical languages and vocabularies necessary to do full justice to the complex expressive, structural, and cultural dimensions of recorded jazz performance.

JEREMY BARHAM
SERIES EDITOR

ACKNOWLEDGMENTS

THROUGHOUT THE PROCESS OF working on this book, I have benefited greatly from the wisdom and generosity of others. The first debt of gratitude must go to my dissertation advisor, Mark Tucker, a great scholar and a good man who was taken from us well before his time. Mark introduced me to a way of thinking about early jazz that took seriously the views of those who created it without dismissing the insights of critics who approached the music from a different perspective—Gunther Schuller, André Hodeir, Lawrence Gushee, and Martin Williams, among others. The dissertation I wrote under Mark's direction laid the conceptual foundation for this book. I only wish he were here to see (and help improve) the final result.

A fellowship from the National Endowment for the Humanities, together with grants from the Jean-Claude Baker Foundation and the School of Music and the College of Fine Arts and Communications at Brigham Young University, made it possible to conduct research in the New York City and Chicago areas. I am grateful to the many specialists and curators who guided me through their collections: Dan Morgenstern and the staff at the Institute of Jazz Studies at Rutgers University–Newark; Michael Cogswell and the staff at the Louis Armstrong House and Archives at Queens College; the staff members of the New York Public Library, Performing Arts Division, and the Schomburg Center for Research in Black Culture; and the staff members of the Chicago Public Library, Woodson Regional location.

While investigating the realm of dance, a field foreign to me, I relied heavily on a number of experts. Again, Mark Tucker pointed the way many years ago, when in the course of advising me on my dissertation he suggested that I watch for connections between trumpet players and dancers. At the time I had no idea what he was talking about. When I finally figured it out and needed guidance, I received help from several remarkable individuals, some of whom performed small miracles on my behalf. Margo Jefferson offered valuable advice at a crucial moment. One of her tips led me to Jean-Claude Baker, who shared so much, including period photographs, financial support (through a grant from the Jean-Claude Baker Foundation), and delicious meals at his restaurant, Chez Josephine. I also owe a debt of gratitude to Pryor Dodge, the son of Roger Pryor Dodge, early jazz critic and eccentric dancer extraordinaire. Pryor was most generous in sharing knowledge and artifacts of his father's legacy. For their help in tracking down information on Brown and McGraw, I am grateful to my friends Mark and Tory Perry, Erlon Hodge of the New York Supreme Court, Margaret Hyson of the Brigham Young University Family History Center, Ernest "Brownie" Brown of the great dance team Cook and Brown, and Lane Alexander and Reggio McLaughlin of the Chicago Human Rhythm Project. Thanks also to Frank Driggs, who provided the only known photo of Brown and McGraw, and to Albert Lawrence, a nephew of Brown and McGraw, who shared his memories with me.

As always with projects like this, I am grateful to friends and colleagues in academia, both at Brigham Young University and elsewhere, for their expert advice, moral support, letters of recommendation, and willingness to read unpolished prose. I would particularly like to thank Thomas Brothers, Samuel A. Floyd Jr., Krin Gabbard, Charles Hiroshi Garrett, Michael Hicks, Steven Johnson, William Howland Kenney, Charles Kinzer, Jeffrey Magee, Lewis Porter, and Kate Van Orden. Scholarship is a lonely calling, and the association of such people provides much-needed camaraderie and a measure of protection from one's historical delusions. Whatever delusions remain in this work, I hasten to add, are mine and mine alone, cherished and coddled day and night in the padded cell that I call my office.

I want to thank Jeremy Barham, editor of Oxford Studies in Recorded Jazz, for inviting me to contribute to the series, and Suzanne Ryan, music editor at Oxford University Press, for her staunch enthusiasm and support. They have been a pleasure to work with from beginning to end. Thanks also to Liz Smith and Karen Fisher, who prepared the manuscript and did the copyediting. At Brigham Young University, Joseph Sowa helped create the musical examples.

Finally, I am grateful to my family—first of all, to my living parents, Herb and Myrna Harker, as well as to my mother, Beryl Harker, who died when I was eight; this book is dedicated to them. My brothers and sisters have been a wonderful source of strength and diversion: Rand Harker, Kim Harker, Scott Harker, Wendy Smith, Val Ellison, and Lori Kilpelainen. As always, I am especially grateful to my wife, Sally, and sons, Daniel and Robbie. Their steadfast love and support are my daily bread, and help me remember what it's all for.

CONTENTS

LOUIS ARMSTRONG'S HOT FIVE AND
HOT SEVEN RECORDINGS

INTRODUCTION

IN JUNE 1924 THE EDITORS OF *The Etude*, a magazine for musicians, surveyed the jazz of their day and made the following historical assessment: "We do know that the Jazz of ten years ago is not to be compared with that of today. Jazz has grown up, gone through high school and is ready for college."[1] The editors were right to see this moment as pivotal in the evolution of jazz, but not—or at least not primarily—for the reasons they supposed. Given a glimpse into the future, they would no doubt have been shocked to learn that the key "professor" to lead jazz through its college years would not be prominent white bandleaders Paul Whiteman or Vincent Lopez, nor composers George Gershwin or Irving Berlin, but a twenty-four-year-old African American cornet player from New Orleans named Louis Armstrong (1901–71). Shortly

---

1   *The Etude* (June 1924): 369.

after this statement was published, Prof. Louis opened school, so to speak, and began to "teach," producing from 1925 to 1928 a series of over seventy 78 rpm recordings for OKeh Records.[2] Featuring Louis Armstrong's Hot Five or his Hot Seven, New Orleans-style groups of varying personnel and instrumentation (sometimes including six members), the records are known collectively as the Hot Fives. Although Armstrong's previous recordings showed remarkable originality, the Hot Fives went much further, redefining jazz and placing it on a new course, one more revolutionary and far-reaching than any subsequent upheavals in the music's history. In particular, the Hot Fives helped change the nature of instrumental jazz in the 1920s, shifting the focus from lively ensembles to lengthy statements by virtuoso soloists. This book attempts to explain, in the most significant senses, how all this came about.

The Hot Five recordings ensued naturally from events set in motion by Armstrong's big break—the call in 1922 to leave New Orleans and come to Chicago to play in King Oliver's Creole Jazz Band at the Lincoln Gardens.[3] In the summer and fall of 1923, Oliver's band recorded for OKeh Records. During these sessions the recording team got a chance to hear Armstrong's playing, and Armstrong became acquainted with E. A. Fearn, the OKeh manager in Chicago, and Ralph Peer, the director of production. When Armstrong moved to New York to play with Fletcher Henderson in 1924, his new wife and de facto manager, Lil Hardin, pressed Peer to record him there. Peer, who later claimed credit for launching the blues craze with Mamie Smith's "Crazy Blues" (1920), saw in Armstrong a potential new star for OKeh's "race record" portfolio. During his time in New York, Armstrong played on several record dates produced by Peer, including the historically important Blue Five records made with Sidney Bechet under the leadership of Clarence Williams. By late 1925 Peer was ready to take the next step. At Hardin's instigation, apparently, he offered Armstrong an exclusive contract to make records under his own name, credited to Louis Armstrong and His Hot Five, as soon as he returned to Chicago. As sidemen Armstrong chose three fellow New Orleanians—trombonist Kid Ory,

2 Speaking of the pedagogical value of these records, New Orleans guitarist Danny Barker recalled that "all the alert jazz musicians and local music lovers waited anxiously for each of Louis Armstrong's latest releases, as there was much to learn from these classics." Danny Barker, *A Life in Jazz*, ed. Alyn Shipton (London: Macmillan, 1986), 42.

3 The best account of the Hot Fives' origins may be found in Gene Anderson, "The Origin of Armstrong's Hot Fives and Hot Sevens," *College Music Symposium* 43 (2003): 13–24; see also Terry Teachout, *Pops: A Life of Louis Armstrong* (Boston: Houghton Mifflin Harcourt, 2009), 91–98.

clarinetist Johnny Dodds, and banjoist Johnny St. Cyr—plus one outsider: his wife Lil on piano. (Although Hardin was from Memphis, her musical background gave her a strong New Orleans pedigree: at age seventeen she had made her professional debut with the pioneering New Orleans Jazz Band, led by Lawrence Duhé.)

With this group Armstrong made twenty-four recordings between November 1925 and November 1926. During the second week of May 1927, he replaced Ory with John Thomas, expanded the band to include tuba player Pete Briggs and drummer Baby Dodds, and recorded eleven sides under the name Louis Armstrong and His Hot Seven. From September to December 1927, he reassembled the original Hot Five to make nine additional recordings, adding guitarist Lonnie Johnson to three tracks. Then, in a sweeping personnel change, Armstrong hired four northern musicians—including the brilliant pianist Earl Hines—and one New Orleanian, drummer Zutty Singleton, to make the last eighteen Hot Five recordings, from June to December 1928 (some of which were attributed to Louis Armstrong and His Orchestra or Louis Armstrong and His Savoy Ballroom Five). To distinguish this last group from the New Orleans Hot Five and the Hot Seven, I will call it the Chicago Hot Five.[4]

Although the earlier bands were assembled strictly for recording, the members had played together a great deal in the past. Armstrong had worked with Ory and Johnny Dodds in Ory's Brownskinned Babies in New Orleans, with Baby Dodds on the riverboats, and with both Dodds brothers and Hardin in Oliver's Creole Jazz Band. The musicians' combined experience in the New Orleans idiom imparted a unity, maturity, and depth to their studio performances that was normally enjoyed only by regular working bands. The Chicago Hot Five, by contrast, was a smaller version of Carroll Dickerson's Savoyagers, the band that Armstrong played with every night at the Savoy Ballroom, and before that, the Sunset Café. Thus, the 1928 records reflect both that band's comfortable working habits and, probably, its nightly repertoire as well.

---

4   All these recordings were made for OKeh. Armstrong made similar records for other companies, though not as a leader. On 28 May 1926, the members of the original Hot Five, billed as Lill's [sic] Hot Shots, recorded three sides for Vocalion under Hardin's nominal leadership. Almost a year later, a Hot Seven–like group called Johnny Dodds' Black Bottom Stompers, featuring Armstrong, the Dodds brothers, Roy Palmer on trombone, Barney Bigard on tenor saxophone, Earl Hines on piano, and Bud Scott on banjo, made two cuts for Vocalion and four for Brunswick. Shortly thereafter, Armstrong recorded three of the pieces from this session—"Weary Blues," "Wild Man Blues," and "Melancholy"—with his own Hot Seven.

By the time Armstrong began the Hot Five series in late 1925, several different approaches to jazz had emerged, including the rollicking New Orleans polyphony of King Oliver, the bouncy homophonic dance music of Jean Goldkette, and the zany musical slapstick of Ted Lewis, none of which emphasized sophisticated, extended solos. On the question of the music's future, most observers looked to a new experimental hybrid of jazz and classical music, introduced by Paul Whiteman and George Gershwin through their joint production of *Rhapsody in Blue* (1924). Conventional wisdom in white circles held that this so-called symphonic jazz would surely produce the music's highest cultural achievements. Black writers took a more ambivalent view of symphonic jazz, vacillating between high praise for the ideals of Western art music and resentment toward Whiteman for his neglect of African American features (and musicians) that made jazz special in the first place. But no one in 1925, it is safe to say, was predicting the rise and influence of someone like Armstrong. First of all, he was a performer instead of a composer, and thus seemed unlikely to determine the conditions for musical change. Black performers, in particular, were thought to be ingenious mimics or clever showmen, but not creators in any deep sense. It was unthinkable that such a person could establish a body of musical principles upon which the next generation of jazz musicians—both white and black—might base their work. And yet virtually all of the important characteristics of 1930s swing, as far as solo playing was concerned, at least, can be traced back to lucidly rendered archetypes in Armstrong's Hot Fives. By the late 1930s Whiteman was considered passé, and Armstrong was just beginning to be recognized for his seminal contributions to the music of swing and, more broadly, the language of jazz.

This much, I believe, is generally agreed upon by jazz historians. What remains to be demonstrated is how Armstrong brought these momentous developments to pass and how observers in the 1920s may have interpreted them. Some stylistic revolutions in the history of jazz—bebop, free jazz, and fusion, for instance—were immediately recognized as such. But Armstrong's was a quiet revolution whose full implications went undetected for a long time, even within the black community. This book will argue that 1920s listeners first understood his Hot Five music not as a major realignment of jazz but in more familiar terms as (1) traditional New Orleans dance music marketed toward black southern migrants (as race records), and (2) a manifestation of novelty entertainment such as one might hear on a vaudeville stage. In the former sense, the Hot Fives extended the same tradition upheld by King Oliver a few years previously and had little to offer the next generation. It was in the latter sense, as music saturated in the values of novelty, that Armstrong's playing most strongly broke with convention. Yet what we, in hindsight, view as his most striking innovations may have come across to 1920s listeners, paradoxically, as par for the course in a world in which the outlandishly new was expected as a starting point for success. Thus, in addition to underrating Armstrong on account of his race, his contemporaries may have underestimated the significance of his playing in purely musical terms as well. The perspective of novelty also tells us something about Armstrong's motivations—why he chose to play in an unusual manner for his time, and what he hoped to gain by it. We will see that in the pursuit of novelty, Armstrong did not create new music out of whole cloth but by reinterpreting materials readily at hand, familiar materials that sounded brazenly novel when catalyzed by Armstrong's uncanny transformative gifts.

Armstrong is widely regarded as an innovator, but rarely does he receive the credit due to him as a consolidator. Over the course of the Hot Five series, and especially near the end, one can sense Armstrong's desire to bring together diverse threads of the jazz and pop music of his day. In particular, it seems clear that he wanted to reconcile the contrasting idioms and agendas of hot and sweet jazz (a project that also occupied Fletcher Henderson, Duke Ellington, Fats Waller, and other black jazz musicians of the period). In doing so, Armstrong prefigured the peculiar stylistic mix that made the most successful swing bands palatable to a large public in the 1930s. Taking from Whiteman and his ilk only what he needed—that is, sweet but not overtly symphonic elements—while preserving as a foundation his own hot traditions, Armstrong changed the rules of the game. Listeners concerned with the quality of jazz (both moral and musical) no longer faced a simplistic choice between the disreputable hot style and the apparently more refined and dignified sweet style. Armstrong made it safe to enjoy both and, as a growing number of contemporary critics recognized, did so at a level of great artistry. His achievement thus opened the way to the marriage of art and commerce in the swing era, in which the music, at its best, pleased both the jitterbugs and the critics. As Jeffrey Magee has argued with respect to Fletcher Henderson, in this sense Armstrong unexpectedly fulfilled some of the aspirations of the Harlem Renaissance to elevate black cultural achievements to a level of parity with those of white society.[5] Had Armstrong

---

5 Jeffrey Magee, *The Uncrowned King of Swing: Fletcher Henderson and Big Band Jazz* (New York: Oxford University Press, 2005).

not accomplished this stylistic consolidation, his influence might have fallen well short despite the brilliance of his innovations.

Traditionally, studies of early jazz have viewed recordings as timeless works of art, treating them from the critical viewpoint of the writer rather than the workaday perspective of the musicians who made them. These studies emphasize the universal genius of the performers and the influence they seemed to have on other players. In recent years, scholars have developed more contextual approaches. The new studies want to show how the original participants viewed their own work and less the impact it had on succeeding generations. This book will try to bridge the traditional and more recent approaches by assessing the meaning of the Hot Fives both in the 1920s and today. I take for granted that Armstrong changed the face of jazz, becoming the revolutionary genius lionized by early critics. At the same time, I would argue, he accomplished this feat not only by following his undeniably voracious muse, but also by responding to stimuli from his native environment, elements that traditional critics have often ignored as commercial intrusions antithetical to his extraordinary gifts. Sometimes, social forces seemed to drive Armstrong's musical decisions; other times, as in the matter of structural coherence, he went against the cultural grain, moving in a clearly different direction from his colleagues. To illustrate both Armstrong's mammoth talent and his environmental dependence, I will blend old-school note crunching with new-school cultural analysis. By combining methodologies, I hope to avoid blind spots in navigating a complex and diverse body of work.

The emphasis on cultural analysis, I expect, will cause no alarm. Some readers, however, may not be happy with my close readings of Armstrong's solos, nor with my occasional use of terminology and concepts associated with Western classical music and the Euro-American tradition of musical analysis. With a twinge of embarrassment, I recognize that Armstrong himself would have rejected the very task I have undertaken—partly out of modesty and partly from a homespun ideology that refused to sully music with logic: "I don't think you should analyze music. Like the old-timer told me,...'Don't worry about that black cow giving white milk. Just drink the milk.'"[6] To potential detractors I can only say that I have tried to ground my analyses in the views of jazz musicians, both Armstrong himself and those who knew him well. If I discuss virtuosity or coherence or harmony, it is usually because musicians brought

---

6   Richard Meryman, "An Authentic American Genius: An Interview with Louis Armstrong," *Life*, 15 April 1966, 104.

up these concepts first. If I use language drawn from European analytical traditions, it is because I know of no alternative systems that address specific musical passages with the same precision. In chapter 2 I make a tentative effort to connect Armstrong's motivic strategies with principles of African American oral rhetoric, while recognizing that such an effort must be regarded as experimental at best. Nevertheless, I operate under the assumption that cultural context has little meaning without a text, and that probing both text and context with equal rigor makes a basic kind of sense (even if such a balance is not always necessary or even possible in writing history). Whether or not I have achieved this objective is another matter.

To accomplish my purpose of charting the peaks, I will not try to conduct an exhaustive survey of Armstrong's many recordings in the Hot Five series.[7] Rather, this book focuses on seven exceptional (and in that sense not necessarily representative) records, treated in chronological order by date of recording: "Cornet Chop Suey" (February 1926), "Big Butter and Egg Man" (November 1926), "Potato Head Blues" (May 1927), "S.O.L. Blues" (and its twin "Gully Low Blues") (May 1927), "Savoy Blues" (December 1927), and "West End Blues" (June 1928). Other records in the series receive less attention, serving primarily as a context against which to evaluate these seven. In a similar vein, I do not say much about ensemble interaction or Armstrong's singing in the Hot Fives, since these matters bear more lightly on my topic. As I see it, his singing had little direct effect on the transformation of jazz in the 1920s from an ensemble-based to a solo-based music. And the collective activity of the Hot Fives was largely a throwback to tradition and had little influence on what jazz was becoming in the late 1920s and early 1930s.

My primary motivation for choosing these seven records has not been to further canonize them. While these records are historically important, I do not see them as static, concrete works that sent unique ripples of influence through the jazz community much as Beethoven's symphonies, say, affected later Romantic composers. Judging from oral histories, it seems likely that Armstrong's disciples learned his music just as much or more from repeatedly witnessing live performances as from listening to his records. "West End Blues," to take one example, was probably

7 For a thorough analytical treatment of all the New Orleans Hot Fives through "Savoy Blues" (though not including the Hot Sevens), see Gene H. Anderson, *The Original Hot Five Recordings of Louis Armstrong* (New York:Pendragon Press, 2007). Useful information can also be found in Edward Brooks's annotated discography, *The Young Louis Armstrong on Records: A Critical Survey of the Early Recordings* (Lanham, MD: Scarecrow Press, 2002).

not a fixed entity but an amorphous, fluid construct that came together in other musicians' minds from multiple performances of that piece at the Savoy Ballroom in Chicago as well as from Armstrong's famous 1928 recording for OKeh. In this sense, these seven Hot Five recordings might be regarded as private snapshots of a dynamic creative process that played out perhaps even more dramatically in public. They give evidence of Armstrong's enormous contributions to jazz but, by themselves, do not constitute those contributions.

I selected these records for their capacity to represent specific stylistic or technical principles. The first chapter portrays "Cornet Chop Suey" as a vehicle for Armstrong's startling virtuosity, particularly his speed and agility, which he himself summed up in the term "fast fingers." This skill initially arose from Armstrong's need to distinguish himself in competition with other young cornet players in New Orleans, but took on a different—or additional—meaning after Armstrong moved to Chicago. To make a good living as a jazz soloist in the North, he had to satisfy the demand for novelty. His employer and mentor, King Oliver, gave him a thorough introduction to novelty, through both Oliver's solos and duet breaks that Oliver and Armstrong played together. As a soloist, Oliver became famous for using muted wah-wah effects to imitate preachers, crying babies, animals, and so forth. In doing so, he maintained a tradition among New Orleans cornetists dating back twenty years, at least, to Buddy Bolden, the legendary founder of jazz. Armstrong, too, wanted to continue this tradition, but for some reason found muted effects difficult to master. So he fell back on the technical fireworks he had been working on in New Orleans. Like Oliver, Armstrong embraced vaudevillian mimesis as his expressive channel, but instead of using wah-wah effects to imitate people and animals, he used runs and arpeggios to imitate the style of New Orleans clarinetists. The longest and most vivid example of this style appears in "Cornet Chop Suey," the introduction of which features cascading arpeggios. Although he subsequently dropped overt "clarinetisms" from his playing, Armstrong continued to develop the acrobatic impulse such references had implanted.

The second chapter addresses one of the most significant of Armstrong's achievements, namely his ability to craft extended, coherent solos based on abstract melodies. Before Armstrong, cornet soloists tended to play paraphrases of a song's melody or very short breaks (unaccompanied solos) on newly invented material. Armstrong was among the first to play lengthy solos on the abstract material characteristic of breaks. More important, he managed to connect the various phrases of his solos, creating a sense of ongoing coherence. In doing so he rejected the prevailing standard of novelty that encouraged a rambling, disjointed rhetoric in order to provide a more or less constant sense of the unexpected. In its place he substituted a structural conception that later musicians would identify with the phrase "telling a story." It was this conception, based on narrative, that would govern most jazz solos of the 1930s, 1940s, and beyond. One of the most impressive early examples of a strongly coherent full-length solo was "Big Butter and Egg Man." Armstrong holds this solo together through a complex network of motivic relationships at multiple levels of phrase structure. The unity relies chiefly, however, on his elaboration of a single melodic kernel that first appears in the fourth phrase. In this regard, despite a high degree of abstraction, "Big Butter and Egg Man" still partakes of the old tradition of melodic paraphrase. To get a sense of Armstrong's approach to solos based on a harmonic progression, we must look to such later recordings as "Potato Head Blues."

Armstrong's ability to play lengthy, coherent solos on abstract material helped shift the focus of the jazz solo from the melody to the harmony, from melodic paraphrases to what Scott DeVeaux calls "harmonic improvisation."[8] This process, treated in the third chapter, required Armstrong to bring arpeggios and runs—which had previously been confined to the fringes of his solos in introductions and breaks—into the body of his solos. One gets the impression that he did not find this an easy task. The broken chords in one of his earliest fully arpeggiated solos, on "Oriental Strut" (1926), come across as a bit forced; as he outlines the chords, Armstrong shows his mastery of the harmonic progression but seems as yet unsure how to turn plain arpeggios into memorable melody. A year later, however, on "Potato Head Blues," he seems to have made a breakthrough. One of his most rigorously arpeggiated solos on record, "Potato Head Blues" also achieves a striking rhetorical fluency and unselfconsciousness. He no longer seems concerned simply to run the changes but instead focuses on making melody out of harmony, unleashing phrase after phrase of lyrical configurations of broken chords. Moreover, the phrases relate to one another motivically, binding the entire solo together in a coherent statement. In this way, "Potato Head Blues" offers a new approach to jazz based on structurally integrated variations of a chord progression rather than embellishments of a fixed melody.

The fourth chapter treats Armstrong's quest for dominance in the upper register of the trumpet. Although classically trained trumpet

8   Scott DeVeaux, *The Birth of Bebop: A Social and Musical History* (Berkeley: University of California Press, 1997), 78–84.

players could match Armstrong's range, their tones became thin as they went higher in pitch. Armstrong's tone, by contrast, became more brilliant in the upper register. During the 1930s, trumpet pedagogues discovered the reason for this discrepancy: in the early twentieth century it was believed that high notes resulted from stretching the lips into a smile, a technique that produced a thin tone. Later, it was discovered that tongue motion actually created the rise in pitch, and that by puckering rather than stretching the lips a player could preserve a full tone in all registers. Armstrong, an autodidact on the trumpet, stumbled onto this powerful way of playing just as classical theorists were beginning to identify it. The first extended example of this new style can be heard in Armstrong's solo on "S.O.L. Blues" and "Gully Low Blues," two versions of essentially the same tune, recorded a day apart. In both solos, at a relatively slow tempo, Armstrong begins the first five phrases with powerfully sustained high Cs. These notes signified a special kind of confidence, displaying a masculine swagger and latent sexuality that colored perceptions of jazz trumpet in the early days, according to Krin Gabbard.[9] The solos also forecast high note techniques that Armstrong and others would more fully develop in the 1930s, such as the half-valve glissando and the shake.

The fifth chapter shows how Armstrong used the blues, the most lowly and disreputable idiom of black popular music in the 1920s, to bring sweet elements into his solo style. Armstrong inherited a blues tradition rooted in the lowdown music of New Orleans, emphasizing loud dynamics, searing blue notes, rough tone color, and similarly "gutbucket" musical traits. Like King Oliver before him, Armstrong mastered this style of playing, as his nearly one hundred recorded accompaniments for blues singers amply attest. Yet these recordings also indicate a restlessness or dissatisfaction with the idiom he had inherited. Seemingly bored with the uneventful harmonic activity of most blues songs, Armstrong began exploring more colorful harmonies as early as 1924. This interest in harmonic color—a characteristic of sweet music—became more pronounced as the decade went on. In 1927 Armstrong became a big fan of Guy Lombardo, a leading exponent of sweet music who began performing in Chicago that fall. It may be no coincidence that at the end of the year, Armstrong recorded a blues piece in a style more obviously indebted to sweet music than anything he had previously recorded. On "Savoy Blues" he uses triadic extensions and rubato rhythms to create

9   See Krin Gabbard, "Signifyin(g) the Phallus: Representations of the Jazz Trumpet," in *Jammin' at the Margins: Jazz and the American Cinema* (Chicago: University of Chicago Press, 1996), 138–59.

feelings of melancholy or nostalgia, a mood far removed from the rough and raucous ethos that had come to define the blues idiom. By bringing together within the framework of the blues elements of sweet and hot, urban and rural, North and South, Armstrong took part in a movement identified by Guthrie P. Ramsey as "Afro-Modernism," which crested at midcentury and pervaded all African American popular genres.[10]

Sweet elements alone did not fulfill Armstrong's aspirations to a more high-class style of playing. The economic need for stylistic versatility required Armstrong to become acquainted with principles of the European classical tradition as well. This phase of his development appears to have intensified during his brief rivalry with trumpeter Reuben Reeves. For months in early 1928, Reeves was lauded in the black press—at Armstrong's expense—for the classical refinement and polish of his jazz playing. The praise came abruptly to an end that spring as Armstrong became a popular star at the Savoy Ballroom. Armstrong's recordings from this period suggest that he bested Reeves on his own turf, by showing a command not only of hot style but also of sweet and even classical references. This is especially clear in "West End Blues," the subject of chapter 6. This piece is regarded as a landmark recording, probably for the astonishing virtuosity of Armstrong's unaccompanied solo introduction. Equally important in my view is the range of stylistic resources he brings to bear throughout the piece. Hot, sweet, gutbucket, classical, clarinet style, and vaudevillian novelty all intermingle in a topical mélange that dismayed New Orleans purists but that must partly account for the recording's broad appeal among young musicians of the next generation. In "West End Blues," Armstrong presented himself as a cosmopolitan sophisticate, not by abandoning his New Orleans heritage but by tempering and integrating it with "high-class" northern elements, just as he had physically integrated with northern musicians in this last edition of the Hot Five.

Indeed, if there is a structural theme that unites the diverse trends in these seven records, it is integration. Proceeding from an early reliance on formulas, Armstrong found a way to dissolve the stock figures and blend their essential qualities into a mature solo language. Thus we see him breaking down clarinet-style arpeggios and deriving from them a more natural and fluid approach to figuration. His initial dependence on ragtime clichés yields to fresh and unpredictable rhythmic patterns. His penchant for playing high C leads to a groundbreaking expressive vocabulary in the upper register. And his fascination with sweet and classical

---

10 Guthrie P. Ramsey Jr., *Race Music: Black Cultures from Bebop to Hip-Hop* (Berkeley: University of California Press; Chicago: Center for Black Music Research, 2003), 27–30.

music opens new vistas, expanding his technique and adding color to his tonal palette without sacrificing the vigor of his original conception. Drawing together elements from the various traditions of his time, Armstrong created something new and whole and prophetic in its implications. In this way, like all great historical figures he summed up an era.

In 1944, an interviewer longing for a return to the old ways asked: "Do you think jazz will ever regain the freshness and the spontaneity and the naturalness of the music as it was played down in New Orleans?" Armstrong's answer must have been disappointing: "It will, but there's always goin' to be some kind of an addition nowadays to polish it up, see, they couldn't afford to play jazz as rough as they did way back in the days of Buddy Bolden and King Oliver.... [Listeners] wouldn't appreciate it, it's gotta be smoothed out some kinda way."[11] In this gentle rebuke, Armstrong rejected the interviewer's cherished ideal of jazz as a pure and primitive folk music untouched by the marketplace. Although this notion has been out of favor for a long time now, its romantic implications remain alive in jazz commentary and continue to shape our interpretation of the Hot Fives. How might Armstrong's achievements appear if considered from another perspective, as his attempt to placate those finicky listeners, whether by smoothing out or, contrarily, galvanizing his idiom? That is the question this book tries to answer.

---

11   Art Hodes and Chadwick Hansen, eds., *Selections from the Gutter: Jazz Portraits from 'The Jazz Record'* (Berkeley: University of California Press, 1977), 82.

CHAPTER 1

NOVELTY
"CORNET CHOP SUEY"

(26 FEBRUARY 1926)

You take an old ham actor like Satchmo, you press
a button and you got yourself a show.

— LOUIS ARMSTRONG

FROM ITS EARLIEST YEARS IN THE great American cities of the
North, jazz appeared in venues modeled on two basic prototypes: the
dance hall and the vaudeville stage. The dance hall and its cousins—
hotel ballrooms, cabarets, and the like—fostered the development of jazz
as dance music, vitally supporting the social dance craze that covered
the nation, in ever-accumulating waves, from World War I through the
crash, the Great Depression, and beyond. This aspect of jazz, the one that
provided rhythms uncannily suitable for dancing, flourished primarily
through the engines of finely tuned ensembles. From the bands of King
Oliver and Paul Whiteman in the 1920s to Benny Goodman and Count
Basie in the 1930s, jazz was, par excellence, a music to be danced to. But
of course it was also more than that. Long before the swing era, jazz was,
in addition, a kind of sonic spectacle—a wonder, an oddity, an exhibi-
tion, a freak act—in short, a novelty. This aspect of jazz, the one weaned
on a vaudeville stage, drawing laughter or slack-jawed amazement from

audiences, flourished primarily through the exploits of inventive soloists. And it is here, with vaudeville, that our account of Louis Armstrong's Hot Fives, the preeminent solo recordings of the age, properly begins.

It is true that during his formative years, before 1930 or so, Armstrong never played in vaudeville, strictly speaking. Yet the same kinds of venues that presented jazz as social dance music often had a floor show. And for most of his major engagements as an up-and-coming player, Armstrong performed stage routines that would have been indistinguishable from the kind of act he might have done on the Keith circuit. Singing, dancing, acting in comedy sketches, wearing silly costumes, horsing around with the audience—such antics formed an essential part of Armstrong's nightly routine in Chicago. In addition to embracing the outward forms of vaudeville, he also absorbed the assumptions, values, and aspirations of other show business people of his day. The very language employed to describe early jazz seems to have been borrowed, in many cases, from vaudeville. Slang words like *hot, pep, legit, novelty, eccentric,* and *freak*; technical terms like *break* and *stop-time*; and notions of high-class and low-class entertainment were all used to describe singers, dancers, and comedians before they were ever applied to jazz. Dave Peyton, the chief music critic of the *Chicago Defender*, urged bandleaders to become "actors" as well as musicians,[1] advice Armstrong took to heart, and not just in the sense that he later made movies. As late as 1966 he described his live concerts in vaudevillian (if not penny arcadian) terms: "You take an old ham actor like Satchmo, you press a button and you got yourself a show."[2]

We should not be surprised, therefore, to find the young Armstrong's handlers treating him very much like a vaudeville rookie shooting for the big time. It is often noted, for instance, that when Armstrong opened at the Sunset Café, the owner, Joe Glaser, put out a sign advertising "The World's Greatest Trumpet Player." Other accounts have Armstrong's wife Lil Hardin posting the sign six months earlier, in front of the Dreamland Café, where Armstrong opened in late 1925. Both stories are probably true. In fact, almost every time Armstrong's name appeared in print in the late 1920s, whether in news accounts or advertisements, it was followed by some version of the tag "World's Greatest Cornetist" or "Trumpeter." Although such hyperbolic self-promotion might have offended later jazz sensibilities, it went hand-in-glove with a career in vaudeville.

1   *Chicago Defender,* 23 July 1927, 6.
2   Jane Margold, "Weekend with Satchmo," *Newsday,* 29 July 1966, 14W. "Louis Armstrong" vertical file, Institute of Jazz Studies, Rutgers University–Newark.

"The big acts all had a catchy handle," one historian wrote, "to help the public remember them."[3] Thus we have Eugen Sandow, "The World's Strongest Man"; Dan Leno, "The Funniest Man on Earth"; Lillian Russell, "The Most Beautiful Woman in the World"; and even Harry Houdini, "The Undisputed King of Handcuffs and the Monarch of Leg Shackles." In this context, Louis Armstrong, "The World's Greatest Trumpet Player," fits right in.

I dwell on the vaudeville connection to counter the powerful, almost suffocating mythology of Armstrong as the first jazz musician in the modern sense. In some respects, of course, he was. But while his early playing style profoundly influenced Coleman Hawkins, Roy Eldridge, and a host of later soloists, it is important to remember that Armstrong did not, could not, envision that legacy for himself in the 1920s. Rather, he worked within the tradition he knew, one that foreshadowed some aspects of the jazz of the future but in other respects differed radically from it. The differences relate principally to a vaudeville sensibility in early jazz that cast individualistic solo gestures as manifestations of novelty. The standard line on Armstrong is that he transcended this sensibility in the Hot Fives by playing solos of compelling artistry unencumbered by tricks. Guided by this perspective, most analysts have sought to understand the Hot Five recordings as they would a solo by Lester Young or Miles Davis—as a chorus of improvised lines tied to a chord progression. The problem is, this latter-day paradigm doesn't always fit Armstrong's early solos. In fact, some of the most striking features can be better explained by reference to the very show business conventions Armstrong supposedly overcame.

This is particularly evident in "Cornet Chop Suey." Arguably the first Hot Five record to portend a new future for jazz, "Cornet Chop Suey" can be seen as a harbinger of trumpet virtuosity in the 1930s. To understand the meaning of this record in the 1920s, however, we should consider it within the context of novelty, a stage tradition that sustained virtually all of Armstrong's cornet-playing predecessors, including his beloved mentor, Joseph "King" Oliver.

NOVELTY FROM THE TOM-JACK TRIO TO KING OLIVER

The first New Orleans jazz bands to play in vaudeville built on the achievements of earlier generations of stage musicians. Beginning in the last decades of the nineteenth century, musical performers divided

---

3   Trav S. D. *No Applause—Just Throw Money: The Book That Made Vaudeville Famous* (New York: Faber & Faber, 2005), 141.

into two camps—straight (or legit) acts and novelty acts, also known as comedy, eccentric, trick, or freak acts. Straight musicians performed light classical pieces and sentimental songs on standard instruments, emphasizing techniques and tonal values of the European classical tradition. Novelty began as the domain of less conventionally skilled musicians, but when it became clear that such acts usually brought in more money, many straight musicians switched to novelty as well.[4] According to veteran monologist Joe Laurie Jr., novelty musicians needed a gimmick, which usually meant playing odd instruments or standard instruments in an odd way. The Tom-Jack Trio made music by throwing snowballs at tambourines, or by clashing swords and shields together in a fencing act. Tipple & Kilmet played on wheelbarrows, the Transfield Sisters on bottles, and Will Van Allen on knives and forks while eating dinner.[5] Meanwhile, players of conventional instruments found their own gimmicks, such as Wilbur Sweatman, who played three clarinets at once, or Toots Papka, who played the mysterious "Hawaiian guitar" with a small piece of steel hidden in his hand.

The public thirst for musical eccentricity made possible the stage careers of early jazz musicians. The Creole Band, the first New Orleans jazz band to perform in vaudeville, joined the Pantages circuit in 1914. Appearing on the scene before their music was even known as jazz, the band specialized in playing standard band instruments in unusual ways, performing "a style of comedy-music all their own," according to the *Los Angeles Tribune*:

> The very instruments assume new personalities. The staid and dignified bass viol does a tee-to-tum, flaps its wings and clarions a challenge to every feathered chanticleer in the corral. The cornet forgets its ancient and honorable origin and meanders madly through the melody, falsetto, throat and chest register, squeaking like a clarinet with laryngitis, jabbering like an intoxicated baboon, and blaring like an elephant amuck. The clarinet squeaks, squawks and squirms, and the trombone, whose business is clawing, becomes a howling musical maniac.[6]

4   Joe Laurie Jr., *Vaudeville: From the Honky-Tonks to the Palace* (New York: Henry Holt, 1953), 65.

5   Laurie, *Vaudeville*, 67.

6   Lawrence Gushee, *Pioneers of Jazz: The Story of the Creole Band* (New York: Oxford University Press, 2005), 99.

If all this weren't enough, the musicians emitted these bizarre sounds "concurrently," a likely reference to the collective improvisation of New Orleans jazz. Why would anyone want to hear such a cacophony? Certainly for its comedic rather than its musical value: this was "music made to be laughed at," declared the *Tribune*.[7] In an industry that cherished comedy above any other value (except money),[8] the Creole Band hit the spot.

In simulating animal cries, Fred Keppard, the band's cornetist, continued a New Orleans tradition of muted novelty playing dating back to the turn of the century. The legendary Buddy Bolden, one old-timer recalled, had "a specially made cup, that made that cornet moan like a Baptist preacher."[9] Sugar Johnny Smith, according to Lil Hardin, "played a growling cornet style, using cups and old hats to make all kinds of funny noises."[10] The tradition climaxed in the early 1920s with the masterful playing of King Oliver, who conjured preachers, crying babies, roosters, and so forth, through wah-wah effects with his cornet and mute. In his method book *The Novelty Cornetist* (1923), Louis Panico, one of Oliver's white "students" and the star soloist of Isham Jones's orchestra, portrayed these devices as expressions of humor.[11] Oliver's own trick playing did not always depend on comedy, but he made the most of every opportunity to get a laugh, especially on his most popular piece, an unrecorded number called "Eccentric Rag." One night while playing this tune he made Bob Shoffner, his second cornetist, the butt of a racially charged joke. "Joe was quite a guy and he would love to kid a lot," recalled clarinetist Barney Bigard. "So Joe took his mute—he was a master with that mute—and told Bob, 'Here's how a white baby cries: "Oooh, oh, oooh, ohwa,"' from that mute. 'Now, here's how you cried when you were a baby, you big black so and so: "Wah, wah, wah, wah."' All the band broke up so they could hardly play, but Bob didn't see anything funny about it."[12]

In addition to creating humor, Oliver's muted playing fulfilled another important objective of the entertainment business: benign deception.

---

7 Gushee, *Pioneers of Jazz*, 99.
8 As Douglas Gilbert put it, "The essence of American vaudeville was comedy." *American Vaudeville: Its Life and Times* (New York: Whittlesey House, 1940), 243.
9 Thomas Brothers, *Louis Armstrong's New Orleans* (New York: Norton, 2006), 43.
10 Nat Shapiro and Nat Hentoff, eds., *Hear Me Talkin' to Ya: The Story of Jazz as Told by the Men Who Made It* (New York: Rinehart, 1955; reprint, New York: Dover, 1966), 94.
11 Louis Panico, *The Novelty Cornetist* (Chicago: Forster Music, 1923), 3.
12 Barney Bigard, *With Louis and the Duke: The Autobiography of a Jazz Clarinetist*, ed. Barry Martyn (London: Macmillan, 1985), 28.

Today, the word *gimmick* carries derisive connotations, especially for jazz, but in vaudeville it represented a positive good if not a professional necessity. The word, which first appeared in print in the *Wise-Crack Dictionary* in 1926, initially meant "a device for performing a trick or deception," and may have begun as *gimac*, an anagram of *magic*.[13] By this definition, Oliver's gimmicks were the various cups, hats, buckets, and bowls with which he performed his amusing mimicry. This style of playing may reflect the black New Orleans practice of "signifying" on cultural elements for humorous or ironic effect and, long before that, the African custom of using instruments to imitate the human voice.[14] Whatever its origins, Oliver's novelty playing fit into a larger entertainment culture in the North that prized mimesis, parody, and illusionism. From magicians and mind readers to male and female impersonators to a multitude of "ethnic" performers (portraying Jews in sallow greasepaint, Irish in red, Sicilians in olive, Negroes in blackface, and so forth),[15] vaudeville thrived on coaxing audiences to suspend disbelief, or at least go along with an appealing fantasy. Even though Oliver performed in cabarets like Dreamland and the Lincoln Gardens rather than on a bill at the State-Lake Theater downtown, his baby cries and farm animal sounds stemmed from the same impulse to beguile audiences with artful deceptions that inspired such leading stars as Julian Eltinge, the wildly popular female impersonator.

Oliver's most celebrated ruse in the jazz literature, however, had nothing to do with mutes. The key gimmick here was Armstrong himself, working as an accomplice. In 1922, shortly after Armstrong arrived in Chicago to join Oliver's Creole Jazz Band at the Lincoln Gardens, the two cornetists stumbled onto a novelty act that musicians would discuss for decades afterward. At the end of an ensemble passage, Oliver and Armstrong would play a harmonized duet break for two measures. Because the breaks changed constantly, it appeared that Oliver was making them up on the spot—which meant that Armstrong must have been telepathic: how else would he know what to play as a harmony part? The two

13 Robert K. Barnhart, ed., *The Barnhart Dictionary of Etymology* (New York: H.W. Wilson, 1988), 432; John Ayto, *Dictionary of Word Origins* (New York: Little, Brown, 1990), 254.

14 Brothers, *Louis Armstrong's New Orleans*, 80–84; Charles Hersch, *Subversive Sounds: Race and the Birth of Jazz in New Orleans* (Chicago: University of Chicago Press, 2007), 132–37; Samuel A. Floyd Jr., *The Power of Black Music: Interpreting Its History from Africa to the United States* (New York: Oxford University Press, 1995), 28, 33.

15 Robert W. Snyder, *The Voice of the City: Vaudeville and Popular Culture in New York* (New York: Oxford University Press, 1989), 111–12.

cornetists cultivated this mystery by developing a system in which Oliver would surreptitiously cue Armstrong just a few bars before the break. As Armstrong recalled, "While the band was just swinging, the King would lean over to me, moving his valves on his trumpet, make notes, the notes that he was going to make when the break in the tune came. I'd listen, and at the same time, I'd be figuring out my second to his lead. When the break would come, I'd have my part to blend right along with his. The crowd would go mad over it!"[16] The trick would not have worked had Armstrong not had terrific ears and lightning reflexes, but mind reading, at least, was not required.

Oliver's "Snake Rag," recorded 6 April 1923, provides an example of how this routine worked in practice, even in the recording studio. Oliver gives his cue four bars in advance, and then at the break plays the same riff while Armstrong plays parallel thirds below (example 1.1). As this example indicates, the cue was a shorthand version of the actual break, which probably means that by this time they had developed a fund of more or less rehearsed breaks that Oliver could spontaneously choose from in the course of performance.

EXAMPLE 1.1   King Oliver and His Creole Jazz Band, "Snake Rag," 6 April 1923, third chorus of the trio, duet break featuring King Oliver and Louis Armstrong.

Despite their obvious kinship with other kinds of vaudevillian sleight-of-hand, the duet breaks were different in one important respect: the trick made sense only to musicians. When Armstrong said "the crowd would go mad over it," he probably meant (primarily) the phalanx of professional

16 Shapiro and Hentoff, *Hear Me Talkin' to Ya*, 104. For a more thorough account of the duet breaks, see Brian Cameron Harker, "The Early Musical Development of Louis Armstrong, 1901–1928" (PhD diss., Columbia University, 1997), 100–109.

white musicians that crammed the area in front of the bandstand night after night.[17] While laypeople on the dance floor might have delighted in the novelty of a harmonized duet in place of the expected solo break, the illusion of Armstrong's telepathy would have been largely invisible to them. As we shall see, such catering to musicians, such fashioning—in essence—of a novelty for elites, would mark Armstrong's own music as well.

CLARINET STYLE

Thus immersed in the novelty world of the great King Oliver, to whom he looked up as a kind of surrogate father, Armstrong initially set out to follow in Oliver's footsteps. In particular, he tried to master the muted techniques favored by Oliver and every other major jazz cornet soloist in the North, including Fred Keppard, Louis Panico, and Paul Mares in Chicago, and Johnny Dunn, Joe Smith, and Bubber Miley in New York. The only problem was that Armstrong didn't have the knack for muted playing. No matter how hard he practiced Oliver's famous wah-wah solo on "Dippermouth Blues," he couldn't get it right. "And I think it kind of discouraged him," Lil recalled, "because Joe was his idol and he wanted to play like Joe."[18] Well, he did and he didn't. From a practical standpoint it made sense to try to learn muted techniques, since they represented the well-worn path to success. At the same time, his failure to do so may have provoked not just discouragement but also a sense of relief, liberating him to pursue a course more suited to his natural instincts, one he had in fact been following already for years. It is a course best understood as the path to "Cornet Chop Suey."

In an interview from 1951, a journalist played the Hot Five recording of "Cornet Chop Suey" and asked Armstrong to comment. Armstrong said nothing of the Hot Fives but, waxing nostalgic, said the record reminded him of his time as a teenager, "when we played the tail gate (advertisings) in New Orleans.... We kids, including Henry Rena—Buddy Petit—Joe Johnson and myself, we all were very fast on our cornets.... And had some of the fastest fingers anyone could ever imagine a cornet player could have."[19] In Armstrong's mind, "Cornet Chop Suey" stood above all

---

17 Armstrong clarified this point in another account: "When the break came it just was there, *and the musicians ate it up.*" Max Jones and John Chilton, *Louis: The Louis Armstrong Story, 1900–1971* (London, 1971; reprint, New York: Da Capo, 1988), 69. Italics added.

18 Lil Hardin Armstrong, "Satchmo and Me," *American Music* 25 (2007): 114.

19 Louis Armstrong, *Louis Armstrong in His Own Words: Selected Writings*, ed. Thomas Brothers (New York: Oxford University Press, 1999), 133.

for fast fingers—the mastery of intricate figurations with which he and his friends competed during cutting contests in the streets of New Orleans. The young players knew their sheer volubility marked a break with the past. One of them noted proudly that the older generation of cornetists didn't play a lot of notes, preferring instead to "linger" on the blues.[20]

Late in life Armstrong elaborated in a surprising manner on the inspiration for those fast fingers. As a young cornetist, he said, "I was like a *clarinet player*, like the guys run up and down the horn nowadays, boppin' and things. I was doin' all that, fast fingers and everything.... I'd play eight bars and I was gone... *clarinet things*; nothing but figurations and things like that.... Running all over [the] horn." As "prima donnas" charged with decorating the upper reaches of New Orleans ensemble texture, clarinetists provided a powerful model for ambitious young musicians. We know that by the late 1910s Armstrong had memorized on the cornet well-known clarinet parts to "High Society" and "Clarinet Marmalade," probably to mine them for material that he could use in cutting contests with his friends.[21] By volunteering that he had played "clarinet things" in his youth—especially when no critics or historians had yet made that charge—Armstrong was also admitting that this was no accidental or unconscious appropriation; rather, it had been a deliberate gambit on his part, a conscious effort to distinguish himself by playing in a nonidiomatic style. In taking this step Armstrong forged his own brand of novelty, one that would serve him well when his muted technique fell short.

"CORNET CHOP SUEY"

Armstrong composed, notated, and submitted "Cornet Chop Suey" to the Library of Congress as a copyright deposit on 18 January 1924, fully two years before recording it with the Hot Five.[22] Thus, the piece properly belongs to the apprenticeship period of Armstrong's career, when he was still playing second cornet for King Oliver. Although the recording varies slightly from the copyright deposit, it retains enough of Armstrong's original conception to appear somewhat anachronistic within the context of the Hot Fives generally, and of his rapidly evolving solo style in 1926 in particular.

20 Brian Harker, "Louis Armstrong and the Clarinet," *American Music* 21 (2003): 138.
21 Harker, "Louis Armstrong and the Clarinet," 140–43. The expression "prima donnas" is Gunther Schuller's. *Early Jazz: Its Roots and Musical Development* (New York: Oxford University Press, 1968), 195.
22 Anderson, *The Original Hot Five Recordings of Louis Armstrong*, 214, 224.

Armstrong recorded "Cornet Chop Suey" near the end of the first wave of Hot Five recordings, a debut that produced ten sides in late 1925 and early 1926. On 12 November he launched the series with three records: "My Heart," "Yes! I'm in the Barrel," and "Gut Bucket Blues." On 22 February he added "Come Back, Sweet Papa." In musical substance and historical interest, these stand as mere throat-clearing exercises alongside the recordings of 26 February, a session that produced "Georgia Grind," "Heebie Jeebies," "Cornet Chop Suey," "Oriental Strut," "You're Next," and "Muskrat Ramble," most of which would become traditional jazz standards.

In the absence of contemporary reviews, it is difficult to know how these records were viewed at the time of their release. Perhaps the most suggestive evidence comes from advertisements in the *Chicago Defender*. The ads portray the records as, above all, music for dancing. Thus, "Cornet Chop Suey" and "My Heart" are "two fox trots as hot as the Chicago fire. Your feet just must go." Similarly, "Muskrat Ramble" is "a fox trot that makes you just up and dance!" Other hints lean toward comedy. The ad for "Big Fat Ma and Skinny Pa," recorded later that summer, extols both danceable and comic virtues of the music: "There's a world of amusement in store for you, when you hear Louis Armstrong sing this comical tune.... You won't know whether to let your feet do their stuff—or just sit down and shake yourself with laughter."[23] Though not advertised as such, "Heebie Jeebies" must have appealed on comedy grounds as well. Featuring Armstrong's (and history's) first extended scat solo—a true vocal novelty—the record provoked Bix Beiderbecke to laugh out loud when he first heard it.[24] Likewise, the verbal banter of "Gut Bucket Blues" and mild bawdiness of "Georgia Grind" seem as much designed to tickle the funny bone as to set feet in motion.

Against this backdrop of dance and comedy music, "Cornet Chop Suey" stands out. If the ad billed the piece as dance music, that's probably because the OKeh marketing team didn't know what else to do with it. Though no less a creature of novelty than the scat solo on "Heebie Jeebies," Armstrong's playing on "Cornet Chop Suey" is clearly not meant to be laughed at. Despite the lighthearted character of the ensemble passages, Armstrong's studious opening cadenza strikes a serious tone (example 1.2, mm. 1–4). It is possible this seriousness was meant ironically, in fun-poking emulation of concert hall rituals, or through the absurdity of juxtaposed opposites: the sober solo introduction followed by the joyous opening ensemble. Lil Hardin's classical piano introduction to "You're

23 *Defender,* 1 May 1926, 6; 3 July 1926, 6; 23 October 1926, 7.
24 Milton "Mezz" Mezzrow and Bernard Wolfe, *Really the Blues* (New York: Random House, 1946; reprint, New York: Citadel Press, 1990), 122.

Next," recorded the same day, might have served a similar purpose. But this comparison only underscores the imposing nature of Armstrong's introduction. Like Hardin's virtuoso passagework, it was meant to impress. Armstrong himself emphasized the concert hall overtones in "Cornet Chop Suey" when he said, with evident pride, that it "could be played as a trumpet solo or with a symphony orchestra."[25]

EXAMPLE 1.2 Louis Armstrong and His Hot Five, "Cornet Chop Suey," 26 February 1926, cornet part.

25 Armstrong, *Louis Armstrong in His Own Words*, 133.

EXAMPLE 1.2   Continued

*) Alternate fingerings (B♭ trumpet key)

All of which highlights the biggest difference from the other records, one often noted in the literature: "Cornet Chop Suey" is a showcase for Armstrong's cornet. Only two other recordings from this early batch—"Oriental Strut" and "Muskrat Ramble"—feature cornet solos of any significance. And "Cornet Chop Suey" goes well beyond these in the extent of the solos. The title of the piece seems relevant here. In choosing it, Armstrong may have signaled not only the prominence of the cornet but also the special nature of his innovations. As a teenager, Armstrong memorized the highly animated clarinet part to the B section of "Clarinet Marmalade."[26] The similarity of this piece's title to "Cornet Chop Suey," with the parallel instrument-food construction, is striking. Could it be that Armstrong composed "Cornet Chop Suey" as a sly tribute to "Clarinet Marmalade," complete with honorary clarinet figures?

Like other showcases, "Cornet Chop Suey" is organized to highlight the soloist. The piece consists of a sixteen-bar verse followed by a thirty-two-bar chorus unusual for its lack of a bridge: AA'A"A'". The chorus breaks down further into eight four-bar phrases, with the first phrase (a) acting as a kind of refrain that alternates with clearly contrasting phrases (b, c, d) that often feature the soloist:

A   a (4)
       a' (4) (last two measures: stop-time break)
A'   a (4)
       b (4) (stop-time solo)
A" a (4)
       c (4) (stop-time solo)
A'" a (4)
       d (4)

Outside the verse-chorus form, Armstrong calls for opening and closing cadenzas and a sixteen-bar stop-time solo after the piano chorus (mm. 85–100). Finally, in the recording (but not the copyright deposit) Armstrong repeats the chorus after the sixteen-bar solo, this time as an embellished lead amid the polyphonic statements of his colleagues on the front line (mm. 101–32). Whereas in the first chorus Armstrong stays close to the notation in the copyright deposit, in the second he seems to be improvising an imaginative paraphrase of the melody. In this sense the second chorus also assumes the character of a solo, albeit an accompanied one.

Laden with solos, "Cornet Chop Suey" certainly looked to the future, but it is possible to overstate its progressive attributes. Copyrighted in early 1924, the piece is downright old-fashioned in some respects. Such Hot Five recordings as "Muskrat Ramble" and "Big Butter and Egg Man" feature complete solo choruses accompanied only by the rhythm section, anticipating modern practice. But "Cornet Chop Suey" emphasizes the limited openings characteristic of the ragtime generation: breaks and stop-time. Even the extended middle solo does not represent the kind of

26 Harker, "Louis Armstrong and the Clarinet," 140–42.

open "blowing space" that would become customary in later jazz. Instead, it has a chord progression different from both verse and chorus and, like the shorter openings, is in stop-time. In the notation Armstrong wrote "patter" over this solo, a fascinating annotation in this context. In the 1910s and 1920s many Broadway songs added a patter section as a third strain after the verse and chorus. Initially inspired by the patter style of singing in Gilbert and Sullivan, a popular song patter often required rapid repeated notes or a degree of rhythmic complexity in the vocal part. In dance band arrangements, a patter played the same structural role while replacing the singing with some kind of ensemble feature over stop-time accompaniment.[27] In the patter to Fletcher Henderson's "How Come You Do Me Like You Do?" (1924), for instance, a clarinet trio holds forth in stop-time. It was this type of instrumental patter, adapted for soloist, that Armstrong employs here. Needless to say, patter solos would not figure prominently in the future evolution of jazz.

It is important to grasp the traditional, even stodgy framework of "Cornet Chop Suey" in order to properly interpret the influence of the clarinet in Armstrong's playing. To be sure, running eighth notes suffuse the piece with the spirit of clarinet style. But the most self-conscious clarinet references, the ones that sound almost like quotations, appear in the brief solo spaces mentioned above: the introduction, coda, breaks, and stop-time passages. In these solos Armstrong often employs arpeggios in sawtooth patterns, a hallmark of New Orleans clarinet style. This figuration abounds in recorded clarinet solos and obbligatos, uniting the otherwise disparate playing of such distinguished performers as Lorenzo Tio Jr., Johnny Dodds, and Sidney Bechet. In its prototypical form, the sawtooth figuration appears as a series of ascending or descending broken chords separated by jags (example 1.3a–b). If a player wanted to increase the energy of the line, he could double the number of jags by cutting the chords in half (example 1.3c–d). To decrease the tension, clarinetists sometimes used a circular version that kept returning to the opening note (example 1.3e–f). This static figure dominates Benny Goodman's famous "Clarinetitis" (1928) and formed the basis of the well-known saxophone melody of Glenn Miller's swing-era standard, "In the Mood." (It also provided the basis for Kid Ory's "Muskrat Ramble," a fact that supports Armstrong's long-standing claim to have composed the piece, given his interest in clarinet figures at this time.)

27 Magee, *Uncrowned King of Swing*, 42–43; Arthur Lange, *Arranging for the Modern Dance Orchestra* (New York: Arthur Lange, 1926), 207–8.

EXAMPLE 1.3 a) Lorenzo Tio Jr., "Bouncing Around," 3 December 1923, transcribed by Charles E. Kinzer; b) Johnny Dodds, "Buddy's Habit," 5/15 October 1923; c) Sidney Bechet, "Cake Walking Babies (from Home)," 22 December 1924; d) Johnny Dodds, "Potato Head Blues," 10 May 1927; e) Lorenzo Tio Jr., "Lou'siana Swing," ca. 18 February 1924, transcribed by Charles E. Kinzer; f) Johnny Dodds, "Buddy's Habit," 5/15 October 1923.

Armstrong's solos with King Oliver reveal a preoccupation with clarinet figurations, which he undoubtedly acquired in New Orleans and brought with him when he came North. On "Chimes Blues" (1923), his first recorded solo, Armstrong fashions two blues choruses around a constant reiteration of the "In the Mood" riff (example 1.4). Another solo from the Oliver period, "Tears" (1923), consists of a series of arpeggiated breaks, most of which exhibit variations of either the classic sawtooth pattern (mm. 3–4, 7–8, 15–16) or the "In the Mood" riff (mm. 27, 31, 33–34) (example 1.5). The third break, the most striking and original of the group, represents an ingenious adaptation of the sawtooth design by filling the jags with ascending triplets (mm. 15–16).

EXAMPLE 1.4   King Oliver and His Creole Jazz Band, "Chimes Blues," 6 April 1923, Louis Armstrong's solo, first half.

EXAMPLE 1.5   King Oliver and His Creole Jazz Band, "Tears," 5/15 April 1923, Louis Armstrong's breaks.

"Cornet Chop Suey," copyrighted just three months after "Tears," multiplies the clarinet references while restricting them to particular moments. The opening and closing cadenzas reveal clarinet style most clearly (example 1.2). As others have noted, the piece begins with a quotation from "High Society," the clarinet test piece that Armstrong memorized in New Orleans. The rest of the introduction consists of a cascade of sawtooth arpeggios in classic clarinet style (mm. 1–4). Armstrong begins with descending figures, then, after reaching the bottom of his range, changes direction and ascends, thereby extending the sawtooth pattern for a full three measures. In doing so, he goes beyond the practice of clarinetists themselves, who ordinarily confined this figuration to one or two bars before switching to another pattern. Armstrong's prolonged adherence gives the line a studied, exaggerated quality, making it, in effect, a parody of clarinet style. Such naked referentiality returns at the end, where Armstrong links two distinctive clarinet figurations—a descending secondary rag pattern (mm. 136–38) followed by the sawtooth arpeggios of the introduction, now ascending to a final, sustained high A.

Clarinet figures in the patter fit into a fragmentary rhetorical scheme encouraged by the stop-time setting. Armstrong presents the solo in clear two-bar phrases marked off by caesuras, sustained notes, and distinct changes in melodic character. The first phrase has the nature of a syncopated bugle call or fanfare (mm. 85–86). The second, in running eighth notes, provides contrast (mm. 87–88). The third phrase, in turn, contrasts with the second, this time through sawtooth arpeggios in clarinet style (mm. 93–94). And the fourth echoes the opening bugle call while ending the entire eight-bar passage with a bluesy cadence (mm. 91–92). The fifth phrase returns to clarinet style more emphatically by stating the "In the Mood" riff three times in succession, thereby doubling the length of the phrase (mm. 93–96). And the sixth and seventh phrases present fluent eighth-note lines that might have been played on clarinet but do not betray the style directly (mm. 97–100). Like the opening and closing cadenzas, the two obviously clarinet-like passages in the patter are conspicuous but transient.

In a similar way, during the melody of the chorus Armstrong uses clarinet figurations only during the solo breaks. In the first break he links the "In the Mood" riff (m. 27) with the beginning of the third "Tears" break mentioned earlier (m. 28; cf. example 1.5). Armstrong plays the next two stop-time passages straightforwardly, as melodies, not solos (mm. 33–36, 41–44). When he returns to these passages in the second chorus, however, he treats them soloistically. The most obvious clarinet reference appears in the last stop-time passage, where he presents a modified sawtooth pattern broken up by eighth rests (mm. 123–24). Tellingly, both stop-time passages begin with vaulting arpeggios, but the figurations do not evoke clarinet style very strongly (mm. 113–14 and 121–22). As we shall see in chapter 3, these examples seem to be part of a transitional phase in early 1926 during which Armstrong was struggling to create an acrobatic style less reliant on the clarinet.

The most transparent clarinet figurations in "Cornet Chop Suey" allow us to guess at Armstrong's intentions. By confining such direct references to brief openings, Armstrong appears to view clarinet style not as a language to be adopted wholesale, but as a gimmick, a vivid momentary diversion—like Oliver's wah-wah effects—with which he could capture fleeting attention in the evanescent manner of all novelty artists. And yet a comparison of the copyright deposit with the recording also suggests mixed feelings on Armstrong's part, as if he may once have aspired, however inchoately, to co-opt clarinet style in toto. Like other lead sheets, most of his copyright deposits from the 1920s show a simplified, skeletal version of the tune as recorded.[28] But, with few exceptions, the notation for "Cornet Chop Suey" is actually *more complicated* than the lines Armstrong played on the recording two years later. In particular, the former contains several running eighth-note passages that Armstrong simplifies—and often clarifies—in the latter (example 1.6). By comparison with the

---

28 See Gene H. Anderson's reproduction and discussion of Armstrong's "Original Hot Five Copyright Deposits" (i.e., through "Savoy Blues"), *The Original Hot Five Recordings*, 213–37.

still very dynamic recording, the copyright deposit seems almost frenetic. A sometimes awkward quality in the notated lines (e.g., mm. 91–92) suggests that Armstrong was straining for effect, perhaps to convey a relentlessly clarinet-like virtuosity. That his take on the piece changed after two years suggests not only a maturation in his ideas but also, perhaps, a disaffection in his view of clarinet style in the purest sense.

EXAMPLE 1.6 "Cornet Chop Suey," a comparison of eighth-note passages in the copyright deposit with their simplified versions in the recording.

As for the more direct clarinet references that remain in the recording, these were an anomaly by 1926. After he moved to New York in 1924 to play for Fletcher Henderson, Armstrong continued using clarinet figurations in breaks on "Go 'Long Mule," "Shanghai Shuffle," take 2 (both 1924), and other pieces. In subsequent years, however, overt "clarinetisms" would gradually drop out of Armstrong's vocabulary, to be replaced largely by more integrated acrobatic melodies that yet bore traces of the clarinet's early influence. In this context, "Cornet Chop Suey" occupies a unique position. Boasting more clarinet figures—both actual and implied—than any other Armstrong solo, this recording represents the peak of his interest in clarinet style.

WHAT DID IT MEAN?

In taking up clarinet style Armstrong found his own brand of musical subterfuge, charting a course not far distant, in principle, from the faux human and animal cries of Oliver, Keppard, Bolden, and the rest. This point brings us back to his friends in New Orleans. When Armstrong moved to Chicago and made good beyond anyone's expectations, one of his old sparring partners back home expressed frustration and resentment at Armstrong's success. Guitarist Danny Barker tells the story:

> Kid Rena was the king trumpet player, and his six-piece band was acknowledged the best in town. On this Sunday afternoon he stood up in the truck and blew his best, but Lee Collins played a half-dozen tunes which were currently popular on records by Louis Armstrong. These trumpet solos were considered phenomenal at the time. Lee stood up in the truck and angrily blew in the direction of Kid Rena *Cornet Chop Suey, When You're Smilin', Savoy Blues*—he blew his solos exactly as on the records.[29]

Overwhelmed by public enthusiasm for Armstrong's music, Rena lost the contest. Unbowed, he criticized his former rival, taking particular aim—if his language is any indication—at "Cornet Chop Suey": "And because Louis was up North making records and *running up and down like he's crazy* don't mean that he's that great. *He is not playing cornet on that horn; he is imitating a clarinet.* He is showing off."[30] Rena's accusation that Armstrong was imitating a clarinet has the ring of a heckler unmasking a magician—

29 Barker, *A Life in Jazz*, 57.
30 Barker, *A Life in Jazz*, 59. Italics added.

"He's got it up his sleeve!"—as if the act of imitation somehow diminished Armstrong's achievement. Rena's point, apparently, was that Armstrong's most dramatic lines in "Cornet Chop Suey" were not as original as they sounded, and he was right. In that sense Armstrong *was* a magician, creating the illusion of strikingly fresh cornet lines when in fact he had borrowed them from another instrument.

Unfortunately for Rena, it didn't matter that Armstrong was "only" imitating a clarinet, because for listeners who recognized that fact the feat itself trumped originality. Plenty of instruments—strings, woodwinds, and keyboards especially—could be made to execute clarinet-like arpeggios with ease. But arpeggios are difficult to play on brass instruments because the move between chord tones often requires subtle adjustments in embouchure, wind column, and oral cavity instead of the simple depression of a finger key. Classical pedagogies aimed at correcting the inevitable problems of delivery, but few black cornetists had access to the training usually needed to acquire such skill. And none of them—from the early 1920s, at least—used arpeggios in his recorded solos in any way comparable to Armstrong's rigorous deployment in "Cornet Chop Suey." As Rena alleged, Armstrong was indeed showing off. Yet his stunt may actually have been most impressive to other musicians, who recognized the idioms. Like Oliver's duet breaks, the act of playing like a clarinet represented an elite kind of novelty, one that required an insider's perspective to fully appreciate.

In his peculiar take on novelty, Armstrong embraced an aesthetics of difficulty that set him apart from his predecessors. Dave Peyton, Armstrong's most consistent chronicler in the 1920s, seems to have recognized this shift. He still used the old words to describe him, preferring the term *eccentric* to the alternatives *novelty, trick,* or *freak.* But Peyton could see that Armstrong offered a new kind of eccentric playing based more on difficulty than on comedy, more on figuration than effects. Commending Armstrong's "weird jazzy figures," Peyton noted that Armstrong "brought us an entirely different style of playing than King Joe [Oliver] had given us." For Peyton, the new style represented a cultural advance toward sophistication, artistry, and proper training. "The style of jazz playing today requires musicianship to handle it," he wrote in 1928. "The beautiful melodies, *garnished with difficult eccentric figures* and propelled by artful rhythms, hold grip on the world today, replacing the mushy, discordant jazz music [of the past]."[31] Of course, the "difficult eccentric figures"

---

31 Dave Peyton, *Defender,* 28 August 1926, 6; 16 April 1927, 6; 27 August 1927, 8; April 27, 1929, 6; 19 November 1927, 6; 23 January 1926, 6; 10 March 1928, 6. Italics added.

adopted by so many cornetists and trumpet players in the late 1920s had been pioneered largely by Armstrong.

In taking up the clarinet idiom and then extrapolating from it a more generalized acrobatic manner, Armstrong separated novelty style from comedy and redefined it for a new generation—one that quickly outgrew the novelty label. By the late 1930s, "Cornet Chop Suey" no longer stood for clever vaudeville tricks. To the contrary, New Orleans trombonist Preston Jackson saw the record as a foretaste of modern jazz, going so far as to equate it with the proto-bop pyrotechnics of trumpet star Roy Eldridge. "There's *Cornet Chop Suey*," he said. "Listen to the record and listen to Roy's records and compare them."[32] In a similar manner, Armstrong himself connected the figurations of his early years with bebop. "I was crazy on doing a whole lot of fancy figurations, like what they call bop today," he recalled in 1966.[33] By then vaudeville was a fading memory, and even Armstrong associated his daring youthful exploits with what followed them rather than with what came before.

In the 1920s, the progressive connotations of "Cornet Chop Suey" may have tied in to race politics and the new spirit of dignity and self-respect that moved through the black community. This connection is symbolized in Armstrong's evolving relationship to King Oliver. As a guardian of tradition, Oliver disapproved of his protégé's new style, urging him to "play the lead, boy, play the lead [i.e., the melody], so people can know what you're doing."[34] Oliver claimed that it wasn't seemly for a cornetist to abandon his role as bearer of the melody to chase abstract "variations," but that was probably not his main objection. As Thomas Brothers has shown, Oliver himself had been known to replace the melody with variations on occasion.[35] More likely, Oliver felt the ground moving under him and couldn't help trying to suppress the coming earthquake. Feeling the same tremors, Lil Hardin did everything she could to intensify them. Marrying Armstrong scarcely a month after he copyrighted "Cornet Chop Suey," Hardin formulated an ambitious campaign to engineer her new husband's rise to success. As we shall see in subsequent chapters, her plans involved not only exposing to the world his dazzling natural talent but also reinventing him musically and socially to meet higher cultural standards. Believing that Oliver wanted Armstrong in the Creole Jazz Band so he could neutralize him as a threat, Hardin urged Armstrong to

32 Preston Jackson, "Swinging Cats," *Jazz-hot* 3 (August–September 1937): 5.
33 Meryman, "An Authentic American Genius," 104.
34 Meryman, "An Authentic American Genius," 104.
35 Brothers, *Louis Armstrong's New Orleans*, 120.

leave. As Armstrong himself probably recognized, it was time—in more ways than one.

Hardin began her rehabilitation project by weaning Armstrong off his old-fashioned New Orleans clothes and dressing him in the latest northern styles. Although he initially resisted her efforts, this transformation carried tremendous cultural resonance for him. Indeed, shortly after arriving in Chicago two years previously, he had been primed for a makeover by the experience of seeing the stage act of dancer and showman Bill "Bojangles" Robinson. Armstrong wrote years later that "the sharpest Negro man on stage that I [had] ever seen in my life" lived up to all his expectations: "He had on a sharp light tan gabardine summer suit, brown derby and the usual thick soul [*sic*] shoes in which he taps.... His every move was a beautiful picture."[36] Just a few months earlier, Bert Williams, the greatest star of black vaudeville in the 1910s, had passed away. Robinson represented a new generation of black stage artists, one that replaced minstrelsy stereotypes with a more dignified and classy performance image suitable to the New Negro of the 1920s. Robinson's progressive style struck Armstrong as an advancement for African American society in general. "To me [Robinson] was the greatest comedian + dancer in my race. Better than Bert Williams." Why?

> I personally admired Bill Robinson because he was immaculately dressed—you could see the quality in his clothes even from the stage Stopped every show. He did not wear old raggedy top hat and tails with the pants cut off, black cork with thick white lips, etc. But the audiences loved him very much. He was funny from the first time he opened his mouth till he finished. So to me that's what counted. His material is what counted.[37]

As a performer who "didn't need blackface to be funny," Robinson was free to dress in a dignified manner, letting his "material"—his actual routine—do the entertaining for him.

As Gary Giddins has written, Armstrong drew inspiration from Robinson's example.[38] To extend this line of thinking, it appears that Armstrong occupied a similar historical position in relation to Oliver as Robinson occupied vis-à-vis Bert Williams. The style of novelty

36 Armstrong, *Louis Armstrong in His Own Words*, 183–84.
37 Armstrong, *Louis Armstrong in His Own Words*, 27–28.
38 Gary Giddins, *Satchmo* (New York: Doubleday, 1988), 76.

cornet playing exemplified by Oliver and his contemporaries, nurtured in comedy, was the sonic counterpart to the "raggedy top hat and tails with the pants cut off." Musicians marveled at the subtleties of Oliver's technique, but audiences mostly appreciated his humorous imitation of crying babies, roosters, and so forth. When Armstrong poured out runs and arpeggios with unprecedented rhetorical force, it was as if the New Orleans sound had been clothed in an immaculate tuxedo, complete with white cane and gloves. Rather than eliciting laughter, Armstrong drew awe and eventually adulation. In this respect he, too, embodied the New Negro ideal. The occasionally self-deprecating, "lowdown" effects of Oliver and his generation reminded of a repressed and humiliating past. Armstrong's clean, agile, flashy style retained black idioms (e.g., swing and the blues) while demonstrating an instrumental prowess previously associated with white players. For all of his own commitment to good old-fashioned novelty, Armstrong thereby sounded a call to the future, a call never before more urgent than in the cascading arpeggios that intro-duce "Cornet Chop Suey."

CHAPTER 2

TELLING A STORY "BIG BUTTER AND EGG MAN"

(16 NOVEMBER 1926)

> The first chorus I plays the melody. The second chorus I plays the
> melody round the melody, and the third chorus I routines.
>
> — LOUIS ARMSTRONG

IN BRAZEN CONTRAST TO THE ARISTOTELIAN ideals of unity
and order in the theater, vaudeville cultivated, in the words of one historian, "an aesthetic of constant surprise brought about through calculated
novelty. In variety [shows], incongruity is cheerfully, flagrantly flaunted.
Its alphabet goes from K to Z to B to R to W—and therein lies its charm."[1]
Writing eighty years earlier, Louis Panico translated this crazy quilt ethos
to music in his how-to manual, *The Novelty Cornetist* (1923). When playing a solo, he writes, one should strive primarily for "variety, inasmuch
as that quality of avoiding monotony and repetition is essential in any
field of entertainment." As a rule of thumb, Panico recommends that
"never more than two measures of similarity be used, proceeding into
a new idea about every other measure."[2] To illustrate, Panico arbitrarily

---

1   S.D., *No Applause—Just Throw Money*, 7.
2   Panico, *The Novelty Cornetist*, 83.

links together sample breaks given earlier in the manual, filling one four-bar phrase, for instance, with Break No. 16 and Break No. 60, in succession (example 2.1). The patchwork quality of the resulting line implies that Panico was more concerned with striking individual ideas than with a coherent solo. The lively but disjointed solos on many early recordings suggest that this philosophy of willful randomness was widely shared.

EXAMPLE 2.1   Louis Panico, *The Novelty Cornetist* (1923), Break No. 16 and Break No. 60 shown in succession to illustrate an effective solo phrase.

For his part, Armstrong surely believed in novelty, as his clarinet-style figurations attest. But in the matter of structural mayhem he, remarkably, did not embrace the practice of his contemporaries. On early recordings Armstrong plays one neatly formed solo after another, even as he—paradoxically—increases the level of turbulence and unpredictability far above that of his peers. This ability to play coherently while at the same time satisfying the show business demand for surprise goes a long way toward explaining what made Armstrong's rhetoric special.

His achievement did not go unnoticed in the jazz community. From the 1920s down to the present day, jazz musicians both black and white have used the language of coherence, if not the word itself, to describe Armstrong's music. Indeed, Armstrong himself took the lead, allegedly describing his approach to improvisation in terms suggesting logical development and progressive expansion: "The first chorus I plays the melody. The second chorus I plays the melody round the melody, and the third chorus I routines."[3] On another occasion he put it differently. According to Doc Cheatham, a young trumpet-playing admirer in the 1920s, Armstrong counseled his fellow musicians to play solos that made sense while retaining their commitment to the unexpected gesture. In doing so he used a now-familiar jazz metaphor:

The things I learned from Louis Armstrong are the things that I heard during discussions that [he] had with other musicians at times. I wasn't in on it, but I was standing back listening. [He'd say:] *try to tell*

---

3   Richard M. Sudhalter and Philip R. Evans, *Bix: Man and Legend* (New Rochelle, NY: Arlington House, 1974), 192.

*a story with your horn....*Don't just go up there and blow something, you know, that you'd—you don't know what you're doing, making a lot of noise....*He said, make a little story out of it. And to present it so that the people will turn around and look and listen.* Cause you can play...a solo in a place where people are drinking and eating, and they don't pay you any mind, they keep on drinking and eating and talking loud. But *you can shock them with something effective,* that will make them turn around and stop, all of a sudden, and listen. That I've never forgot.[4]

As Paul Berliner has shown, jazz musicians use the phrase "telling a story" to describe a process of sequential unfolding in a solo, a notion presupposing concern for "matters of continuity and cohesion."[5] This folksy expression suggests less quantifiable elements as well, such as personality traits and cultural resonances.[6] But purely musical coherence may be more fundamental. Once during a blindfold test, Armstrong appeared to use the phrase in this sense: "That clarinet is trying to tell a story. You can *follow* him."[7] Trumpeter Roy Eldridge, in describing Armstrong's own playing, even more explicitly connected the idea of telling a story with syntactic continuity and cumulative development: "Every phrase [Armstrong played] led somewhere, linking up with the next one, in the way a storyteller leads you on to the next idea. Louis was *developing* his musical thoughts, moving in one direction. It was like a plot that finished with a climax."[8] This might sound like a conception modeled on European aesthetics, but according to Cheatham, Armstrong's motivation stemmed from his show business environment: he wanted to craft a rhetoric powerful enough to quiet patrons in a noisy nightclub.

Eldridge was not the only one to hear the logic of Armstrong's playing. Bix Beiderbecke and Esten Spurrier, young white musicians who regularly attended Chicago's Lincoln Gardens in 1922–23 to hear Armstrong

4   Jazz Oral History Project, interview with Adolphus "Doc" Cheatham, April 1976, Chris Albertson, interviewer, Institute of Jazz Studies, Rutgers University–Newark. Italics added.

5   Paul F. Berliner, *Thinking in Jazz: The Infinite Art of Improvisation* (Chicago: University of Chicago Press, 1994), 201–5; quote on p. 202.

6   Vijay Iyer, "Exploding the Narrative in Jazz Improvisation," in *Uptown Conversation: The New Jazz Studies,* ed. Robert G. O'Meally, Brent Hayes Edwards, and Farah Jasmine Griffin (New York: Columbia University Press, 2004), 393–403.

7   Armstrong, *Louis Armstrong in His Own Words,* 165.

8   Lewis Porter and Michael Ullman with Edward Hazell, *Jazz: From Its Origins to the Present* (Englewood Cliffs, NJ: Prentice Hall, 1993), 168. Italics added.

play with King Oliver's Creole Jazz Band, recognized that Armstrong "departed greatly from all cornet players…in his ability to compose a close-knit, individual 32 measures with all phrases compatible with each other." Such organization produced, in their words, "correlated choruses." Using language similar to Eldridge's, Spurrier elaborated on this idea: "Bix and I always credited Louis as being the father of the correlated chorus: play two measures, then two related, making four measures, on which you played another four measures related to the first four, and so on…to the end of the chorus." Contrary to Panico's formula, Armstrong presented "a series of related phrases."[9]

This relatedness pertains to musical rhyme, an idea that Ralph Ellison may have intended when he praised Armstrong's "rowdy poetic flights."[10] It is tempting to hear Armstrong's rhyming phrases as an unconscious extension of the rich rhetorical heritage of black vernacular speech. From the venerable practices of sounding, signifying, toasting, and playing the dozens to modern-day rap and hip-hop, rhyme has played a vital role in the cadenced delivery of black street poetry. The notion of rhyme also fits well with storytelling, our other guiding metaphor, for such African American poetic genres as rapping and toasting were built around the framework of narrative.[11] King Oliver loved to play the dozens, and Armstrong himself was well known for his inventive mastery of vernacular slang. It makes sense to think of his musical language as drawing upon the ritualized verbal syntax he grew up with and used every day.

Particularly suggestive is the tradition of playing the dozens in rhymed couplets.[12] One can hear something analogous in Armstrong's playing as early as 1923, in his solo on "Tears." On this tune, as we have seen, Armstrong plays a series of breaks that alternate every two measures with ensemble passages. Yet some of the breaks he binds together motivically as though they were simply successive phrases in a chorus-length solo. The second break, for example, mirrors, parallels, or "rhymes with" the first break in a number of ways: it begins on the second beat; it inverts the sawtooth contour from descending to ascending; and it reverses the sequence of events, placing the running eighth notes in the first bar and the sustained note in the second (example 2.2). But the strongest link

9   Sudhalter and Evans, *Bix*, 51, 100–101.
10 Ralph Ellison, *Shadow and Act* (New York: Random House, 1964), 192.
11 Onwuchekwa Jemie, ed., *Yo' Mama! New Raps, Toasts, Dozens, Jokes & Children's Rhymes from Urban Black America* (Philadelphia: Temple University Press, 2003), 40–59.
12 William Labov, *Language in the Inner City: Studies in the Black English Vernacular* (Philadelphia: University of Pennsylvania Press, 1972), 307–8.

with the first break is in the last five notes. Here the rhythms, contour, minor mode, and final whole step interval are identical, and even the pitches are never farther than a whole step away from their counterparts in the first break. By reserving the strongest similarities for the end of the phrase, Armstrong creates a musical rhyme not unlike that which binds together two lines of poetry. The "rowdiness" referred to by Ellison comes both from Armstrong's rollicking delivery and, in structural terms, from the complex network of internal relationships—secondary rhymes, one might say—prior to the closing five notes.

EXAMPLE 2.2   King Oliver and His Creole Jazz Band, "Tears," musical rhyme between Louis Armstrong's first two breaks.

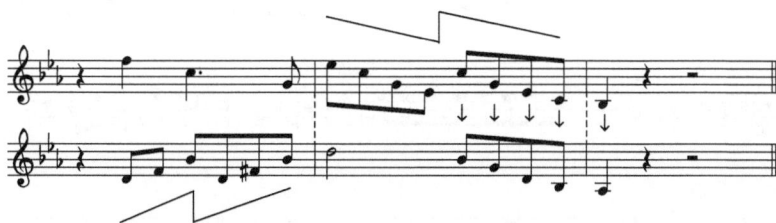

Rhyme and rowdiness, symmetry and surprise: in a structural sense, one can interpret Armstrong's early musical development as a struggle to balance these conflicting impulses. This effort was complicated by his parallel quest to transfer the excitement and ingenuity of the break to the full-length solo, a project that would be vital in leading jazz from its communal origins to its soloistic maturity. Though Armstrong seemed incapable of playing an incoherent solo, the fine-grained correspondences between the first two breaks on "Tears" do not often appear in the body of his extended solos before 1926. "Chimes Blues," as we have seen, is all rhyme in its constant repetition of a single five-note motive. The patter solo in "Cornet Chop Suey" leans to the other extreme, emphasizing contrast and difference; Armstrong provides unity chiefly through the two long notes that end almost every phrase. Playing for Fletcher Henderson in 1924, Armstrong struck a happy medium on "Go 'Long, Mule," a solo featuring the alternation of two basic ideas—"a syncopated figure (emphasizing upbeats) and an unsyncopated figure (emphasizing downbeats)"—together with a razzle-dazzle clarinet-style break in the middle of the chorus.[13] In this solo two rhymes are at work, one connecting the odd measures and another

13 Magee, *Uncrowned King of Swing,* 77.

the even (example 2.3). In contrast to the predictability in "Chimes Blues," however, the repeating motives in "Go 'Long, Mule" sparkle with variational interest.

EXAMPLE 2.3   Fletcher Henderson and His Orchestra, "Go 'Long Mule," Louis Armstrong's solo.

Despite the obvious effectiveness of "Go 'Long, Mule," it seems clear that Armstrong was working under certain structural constraints. A survey of his rhythmic patterns from 1923 to 1925 shows that he greatly preferred a small handful over all the rest. In his solos on "Froggie Moore," "My Rose Marie," "Tell Me, Dreamy Eyes," "Go 'Long, Mule," "Words," "I Miss My Swiss," "Naughty Man," "Copenhagen," "Shanghai Shuffle," "Cake Walking Babies (from Home)," "Why Couldn't It Be Poor Little Me?," "Money Blues," and "Alabamy Bound," three rhythmic patterns occur again and again (table 2.1). These patterns appear to be holdovers from the ragtime generation.[14] Most common is what I call the *Oliver rhythm*, a pattern favored by King Oliver consisting of three quarter notes starting on beat one. This pattern, first noted by Gunther Schuller,[15] appears at least twenty-four times in these solos, twenty more times in variant forms. The second most common is the *cakewalk rhythm*, a short-LONG-short-LONG-LONG pattern that

---

14 The following discussion of rhythmic patterns was inspired by Jeffrey Magee's insightful treatment of black topics in "'Everybody Step': Irving Berlin, Jazz, and Broadway in the 1920s," *Journal of the American Musicological Society* 59, no. 3 (2006): 698–715.

15 Schuller, *Early Jazz*, 94.

governs popular song refrains from the turn of the century such as "Hello! Ma Baby" and "Under the Bamboo Tree." Armstrong uses the cakewalk rhythm (characteristically with a subdivided third beat) twenty-two times, with eleven variants. And the third most common is *two-note secondary rag*, an alternation of quarter notes and eighth notes, creating hemiola in 4/4 time. This pattern appears seventeen times with three variants. These three patterns appear as archetypes in Armstrong's thinking; others recur so infrequently that their repetitions might be coincidental. Seen in this light, the motivic contrast in "Go 'Long, Mule" actually consists of an alternation between the Oliver rhythm and the cakewalk rhythm (and their variants). Despite the variety of pitch and rhythm, it seems clear that Armstrong is still thinking—as with "Chimes Blues" and the patter solo on "Cornet Chop Suey"—in one- and two-measure blocks. The patterns stand apart from one another like tiles in a mosaic rather than being knit together in an integrated and flexible rhythmic language.

Armstrong's use of rhythmic patterns raises the question of "formulaic improvisation." In 1974 Thomas Owens showed how Charlie Parker used short melodic formulas again and again in his solos.[16] Can Armstrong's practice be related to that of Parker and other postwar improvisers? To some extent, yes, but mostly no. Armstrong had a few licks that he played note-for-note in different contexts—the third "Tears" break, for example, shows up again in "Potato Head Blues" (1927)—but this was not his usual modus operandi. Instead, he based his formulas on more fluid constellations of pitch and rhythm. The close family

TABLE 2.1 Three common rhythmic patterns in Louis Armstrong's early solos.

a) Oliver rhythm

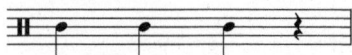

b) Cakewalk rhythm

1. Original   2. Armstrong's preferred version

c) Two-note secondary rag

16 Thomas Owens, "Charlie Parker: Techniques of Improvisation" (PhD diss., University of California, Los Angeles, 1974).

resemblances among the even-numbered measures in "Go 'Long, Mule" show that Armstrong had a conceptual template in mind centered on the cakewalk rhythm and various oscillating pitch patterns, creating melodies that rock back and forth within the interval of a second, third, or fourth. The same relationship between pitch and rhythm appears in "Cake Walking Babies (from Home)," recorded three months later. Here, the rocking figures from "Go 'Long, Mule" beginning with C#–D (mm. 6, 13) reappear in very similar fashion no less than six times (bracketed in example 2.4). Again, the cakewalk rhythm (and, once, two-note secondary rag) seems to provide the rhythmic basis for variation, and the idea of oscillation the melodic basis. The repetition of these melodic-rhythmic modules imparts a sort of unity, but the modular design also undermines full syntactic integration (i.e., the richness and fluency of the storytelling voice) and opposes the much-vaunted element of surprise. At least, judging from changes made in his recordings of the next few years, that is what Armstrong seemed to think.

EXAMPLE 2.4   Clarence Williams's Blue Five, "Cake Walking Babies (from Home)," 8 January 1925, Louis Armstrong's solo.

Beginning with the Hot Five recordings of early 1926, Armstrong tried to break free of the formulaic practices of his time with Oliver and Henderson. One reason may be that he wanted to leave the melodic paraphrase style of the earlier period and play solos based more directly on the harmony. In chapter 3 we will see the consequences of these efforts in such Hot Five solos as "Muskrat Ramble" and "Oriental Strut." Suffice it to say, for now, that it would be November before Armstrong showed a genuine freedom from formulaic constraints. For in that month he recorded "Big Butter and Egg Man from the West," a piece that critics have hailed for its surprising, even unprecedented, structural integrity. The French critic André Hodeir calls it "the first example of a typically individual esthetic conception to be found in the history of recorded jazz."[17] Lawrence Gushee hears in the solo "a degree of linear integration not previously achieved on record."[18] Gunther Schuller sees it "effectively consolidating [Armstrong's] experiments of the preceding years," bringing his "personal trademarks" (read: formulas), which had previously "stood out amid otherwise bland playing," into the service of a "total, unified conception."[19] In "Big Butter and Egg Man," the richly textured cross-references from the first two breaks on "Tears" are successfully transferred to the full-length solo.

17 André Hodeir, *Jazz: Its Evolution and Essence*, trans. David Noakes (New York: Grove Press, 1956), 57.
18 Lawrence Gushee, "The Improvisation of Louis Armstrong," in *In the Course of Performance: Studies in the World of Musical Improvisation*, ed. Bruno Nettl with Melinda Russell (Chicago: University of Chicago Press, 1998), 305.
19 Schuller, *Early Jazz*, 102–3.

The recording session that produced "Big Butter and Egg Man" was preceded in the summer by two sessions generally regarded as far less successful. On 16 June the band recorded four novelty tunes—"Don't Forget to Mess Around," "I'm Gonna Gitcha," "Dropping Shucks," and "Who'sit"—that Schuller considers the "nadir" of the Hot Five series. Similarly, Gene H. Anderson views the next batch, recorded on 23 June— "The King of the Zulus," "Big Fat Ma and Skinny Pa," "Lonesome Blues," and "Sweet Little Papa"—as "the 'worst' of the Hot Fives," although his scare quotes would seem to soften that assessment, and "Sweet Little Papa" garners praise from both Schuller and Anderson.[20] Certainly, such epithets as *nadir* and *worst* assume a standard of artistry that Armstrong and his colleagues probably did not intend. As vehicles of entertainment, these eight recordings may have served their purpose as well as most others in the series. Nevertheless, for our purposes—that is, as a measure of Armstrong's contributions to jazz solo style—they have little to communicate. Although Armstrong sings a great deal (probably, as Anderson suggests, to capitalize on the success of "Heebie Jeebies"), he plays cornet solos on only two numbers, "King of the Zulus" and "Sweet Little Papa." The former is inconsequential, and the latter, though admirably wide-ranging, is derivative, resurrecting an entire four-bar phrase from the patter solo on "Cornet Chop Suey." Most of the fall recordings continue in this unremarkable vein. On 16 November Armstrong recorded, besides "Big Butter and Egg Man," three other tunes: "Jazz Lips," "Skid-Dat-De-Dat," and "Sunset Café Stomp." On 27 November the band followed up with two more: "You Made Me Love You" and "Irish Black Bottom." With the exception of the haunting and harmonically interesting "Skid-Dat-De-Dat," Armstrong's performances on these recordings seem merely adequate to the task, occasionally sounding either perfunctory (e.g., "Sunset Café Stomp") or half-baked (e.g., "Jazz Lips"). Against this gray backdrop, "Big Butter and Egg Man" comes as a stunning development, a bolt from the blue.

"Big Butter and Egg Man" must be understood within the context of Armstrong's lengthy tenure at the Sunset Café, where he had played nightly with Carroll Dickerson's Orchestra since May. Percy Venable, the producer of floor shows at the Sunset, wrote "Big Butter" for Armstrong to perform with singer Mae Alix, probably in connection with one of

20 Schuller, *Early Jazz*, 102; Anderson, *The Original Hot Five Recordings of Louis Armstrong*, 97.

Venable's revues from that fall—*Sunset Affairs, The Sunset Joymakers,* or *Sunset Café Revue.*[21] In 1920s parlance, a "butter and egg man" was a big spender. The term was coined by New York nightclub owner Texas Guinan as a tribute to a high-flying dairy man who frequently visited the El Fey Club. Somehow the newspapers picked it up, and the man's handle, the Big Butter and Egg Man, entered the slang of the nightclub set. (George S. Kaufman memorialized the man in a play, *The Butter and Egg Man,* which opened on Broadway on 23 September 1925, not quite a year before Armstrong made his recording.)[22] Pianist Earl Hines recalled that at the Sunset, Alix "would throw her arms around [Armstrong's] neck and sing, 'I need a Big Butter and Egg Man.' He would stand there and almost melt...and the whole house cracked up."[23]

As far as we know, few of the Hot Five recordings to this point had anything to do with Armstrong's nighttime engagements. With the notable exception of "Heebie Jeebies," most were original New Orleans-style pieces composed especially for the recording sessions, and received almost no exposure in live performances. But the tremendous popularity of "Big Butter and Egg Man" at the Sunset, judging from reminiscences of contemporaries, probably convinced Armstrong to issue a recorded version, together with another Sunset piece—"Sunset Café Stomp"—on side B. Armstrong's Hot Five sidemen replaced the Sunset musicians, except for Alix, at the recording session. The recording, long a favorite among aficionados of early jazz, reveals a happy, easygoing piece in medium tempo and ABCA thirty-two-bar song form; the arrangement consists of four and a half choruses, plus a brief transition before Armstrong's trumpet solo.

Some aspects of the live performance found their way onto the recorded version, including the comic banter between Alix and Armstrong ("Now, momma, I'm your big butter and egg man! But I'm different, honey—I'm from way down in the South!"), and Armstrong's trumpet solo immediately following. It is impossible to know how the recording might have differed from the live version. Perhaps during ensemble passages the Hot Five's New Orleans-style, semi-improvised polyphony replaced a more rehearsed, homophonic arrangement that had been used at the Sunset. Or perhaps, to stay within the roughly three-minute limit of the 78 rpm

21 Stanley Dance, *The World of Earl Hines* (New York: Scribner's, 1977), 49; Scrapbook #83, Louis Armstrong Archive; Anderson, *The Original Hot Five Recordings of Louis Armstrong,* 124.

22 Louise Berliner, *Texas Guinan: Queen of the Nightclubs* (Austin: University of Texas Press, 1993), 101.

23 Dance, *The World of Earl Hines,* 49.

recording format, Armstrong may well have eliminated a few "live" choruses in the studio. We can be reasonably sure, however, that many months of performing the piece had polished and refined Armstrong's trumpet solo. As I have argued elsewhere, multiple takes with Fletcher Henderson indicate that Armstrong perfected his solos over time, repeating them essentially note for note at each new performance.[24] In a similar way, the solo on "Big Butter and Egg Man" had in all likelihood become set, a fixed composition, by the time it was recorded. One night at the Sunset Armstrong invited white cornetist Muggsy Spanier to sit in on the piece. Spanier played Armstrong's solo note for note, later explaining that since "no one in the world can improve on the way he plays it…I'm frank to say that as nearly as possible (because I heard him play it so much and listened so intently) I've always tried to do those famous breaks as Louis did them."[25] Spanier's language here implies that he heard the solo repeatedly in live performances, not on a record.

The many months of refinement may account for the recorded solo's striking sense of integration. In contrast to the solos with Oliver and Henderson, and even some of the early Hot Fives, lengthy rhythmic patterns no longer dominate Armstrong's rhetoric. In "Big Butter" there is one appearance of the Oliver rhythm, three snatches of two-note secondary rag, and none of the cakewalk (bracketed in example 2.5a). Only the last example of two-note secondary rag has the sound of a fixed module, a rhythm in quotation marks, so to speak, that one hears so often in Armstrong's earlier solos.[26] The first two hints of this pattern go by almost unnoticed because they appear as threads deftly woven into longer phrases. Indeed, the first of these phrases (mm. 8–12) illustrates the degree to which Armstrong had forsaken his modular approach. This passage is a model of rhythmic unity within diversity. Armstrong holds the phrase together with a recurring long note—a dotted quarter that appears four times (including a syncopated *pop-pop* variant in mm. 10–11) at intervals of about one measure (example 2.5b). But between these repetitions there is almost constant variability. One gets the impression of a fully integrated rhythmic language that cannot be broken into discrete modules.

24 Brian Harker, "'Telling a Story': Louis Armstrong and Coherence in Early Jazz," *Current Musicology* 63 (1999): 51–58.

25 Shapiro and Hentoff, *Hear Me Talkin' to Ya*, 116–17.

26 Perhaps this is the moment André Hodeir was referring to when he cited "the barely perceptible wavering at the end of the BIG BUTTER chorus; can't we suppose that it was due, ironically enough, to Louis's being obliged, as leader, to let the vocalist know it was time for her to come back on?" Hodeir, *Jazz*, 58.

EXAMPLE 2.5 Louis Armstrong and His Hot Five, "Big Butter and Egg Man," 16 November 1926: a) Louis Armstrong's solo; b) recurring dotted quarter-note values in the fifth phrase.

*) Alternate fingerings (B♭ trumpet key)

The unifying element in this phrase—the recurring dotted quarter note value—shows how Armstrong changed his approach. Instead of relying on long patterns lasting a measure or more, he now repeats shorter elements of two beats or less. The shorter the pattern, the less it sounds like a stock figure or cliché. It tends to merge into its surroundings, not entirely losing its identity or going by unnoticed but becoming part of a larger gesture that thereby takes on new prominence. The dotted quarter notes in example 2.5b unify the music much like the repeating patterns in "Cake Walking Babies" but, being shorter, impart a more subtle coherence, one requiring greater attention on the part of the listener. To take another example, the rhythm of the first three notes in "Big Butter" ♪♩♪ appears frequently throughout the solo; but we don't hear this motive as a "mix-and-match" building block in the same sense as we do, say, the cakewalk rhythm. Not only is it too short, but Armstrong uses it differently. For the first half of the chorus he approaches this motive as an exercise in variable anacruses: we move from the original (mm. 0, 4) to a modified version in four eighth notes (mm. 2, 8) to an expanded version (m. 6), to a contracted version (m. 12), to one splintered into six eighth-note triplets (m. 16). Then, as if to compensate for the digression, Armstrong returns to the original motive, emphatically stating it four times without variation (mm. 20–22). This is the phrase that morphs into two-note secondary rag, which we completely overlook; the pattern's stock identity has been subordinated to its role in the larger phrase, which culminates a still-larger rhythmic trajectory tracing back to the opening measure.

Tellingly, just as Armstrong's rhythms become freer, so do his melodies. In stark contrast to the constrained oscillations in "Cake Walking Babies," the "Big Butter" solo opens with a series of graceful melodic shapes that unfold to even more expansive and elegant structures. As Schuller rhapsodized, "No composer, not even a Mozart or a Schubert, composed anything more natural and inspired."[27] By the same token, at the rhythmically weakest part of the solo, where he lapses into two-note secondary rag (mm. 29–30), Armstrong also reverts to the static rocking pitches we saw in "Cake Walking Babies." To be sure, the qualitative difference between the two solos could be partly attributed to the difference in tempo ("Cake Walking Babies" is much faster) and to the fact that Armstrong probably improvised the solo on "Cake Walking Babies"[28] but worked out "Big Butter" in advance. This can hardly account for the scope of the changes, however, which seems to reflect a difference in kind as well as degree.

THE FREEDOM FROM FORMULAS APPEARS to have liberated Armstrong to weave strands of the solo together—to tell his story, so to

27 Schuller, *Early Jazz*, 104.

28 Two weeks previously, on 22 December 1924, Armstrong had recorded "Cake Walking Babies" with essentially the same group of musicians (though the vocalists were different and the bands went by different names—the Red Onion Jazz Babies in December, Clarence Williams's Blue Five in January). Because his lines throughout this recording are so different from those of the later one, we can assume that both performances were largely improvised.

speak—with unaccustomed subtlety. "When I blow I think of times and things from outa the past that gives me a image of the tune," he once said. "A town, a chick somewhere back down the line, an old man with no name you seen once in a place you don't remember.... What you hear coming from a man's horn—that's what he is."[29] As mentioned earlier, Armstrong's telling of these "stories" from his past took the syntactical form of dramatic poetry. Eldridge heard the stories in terms of narrative plot, complete with complication and denouement. Beiderbecke and Spurrier, on the other hand, heard "correlated choruses" in which each phrase would echo a preceding phrase, a notion suggesting musical rhyme. Both elements—the dramatic and the poetic—figure strongly in "Big Butter and Egg Man."

In the following analysis, I will propose various ways of hearing structural relationships in the solo. Let's begin with the first sixteen measures, the AB sections of the form. Armstrong plays four two-bar phrases, then two four-bar phrases, making six phrases in all (example 2.6). The opening may be heard as a call-and-response, with the first three phrases sounding the call and the fourth the response. One might even hear a question and answer. The insistent repetition, ascending contour, restless rhythms, and roving vibrato of the calls connote uncertainty, while the change of harmony every two measures suggests that the question is being constantly restated. And the response—with its "rip" to the top-line F, inverted contour, precipitous descent, and downward octave transfer of the primary structural pitch A—supplies a decisive answer. In addition, the move from the repeated As (mm. 1–5) to G–F (m. 7) gives a 3̂–2̂–1̂ tonal resolution, underscored by the return of F major in the harmony.

The sense of call-and-response between the two four-bar phrases suggests an antecedent-consequent relationship (example 2.6b). Figures common to both phrases appear at the anacruses (the sixth phrase simply drops the last two eighth notes), the beginnings (mm. 9 and 13, beats 1–2), and especially the endings (mm. 11 and 15, beats 3–4). The registral identity and melodic affinity of the two endings bind the phrases together even more strongly than the four eighth notes. In particular, the down-up pattern of the figure in m. 15 counterbalances the down-down pattern in m. 11, just as the rising minor third (boosted by a chromatic appoggiatura) complements the falling minor third by filling in its spaces.

29 Larry L. King, "Everybody's Louie," *Harper's Magazine* (November 1967): 69.

EXAMPLE 2.6   "Big Butter and Egg Man," opening six phrases of Louis Armstrong's solo.

Armstrong creates other relationships, however, that cut across the phrase divisions in example 2.6. To discover them, it will help to consider Armstrong's paraphrase of the original melody, which—surprisingly— becomes stronger as he goes along (example 2.7). The first five measures echo the melody by dwelling on A, but the contour of the lines would not suggest a resemblance. Yet, as Lawrence Gushee has shown, starting at the end of m. 9 the paraphrase becomes more strict in pitch and contour.[30] And Armstrong's final phrase (mm. 13–15) is a recognizable variant of the corresponding phrase in the melody—far more recognizable than his opening lines. The melody in mm. 14–16, in fact, outlines a melodic kernel (a descending pentatonic scale: A–G–F–D–C) that shapes the entire opening sixteen measures of Armstrong's solo. Armstrong's opening, then, is indeed a paraphrase, but of the melodic kernel in retrograde (minus the G). After three subtly varied statements of this backward version, Armstrong presents three compensating phrases in the forward position (example 2.8a). Whereas in the backward version he omits the G, in the forward version he adds to the kernel an auxiliary note E between A and G. The forward phrases successively fill in the pitches of the kernel: the fourth phrase includes A–E–G–F; the fifth

30 Gushee, "The Improvisation of Louis Armstrong," 305.

phrase, A–E–G–F–D; and the sixth, A–E–G–F–D–C. That this six-pitch kernel truly governs the AB section of the solo is confirmed by its reappearance in its clearest, most concise form at the return of A, immediately after the bridge (example 2.8b). Armstrong's approximately reverse approach to his material—choosing a melodic fragment from the end of a section, beginning with retrograde forms, and saving the most transparent paraphrase for the end of the solo—counters traditional assumptions that jazz variations move from the familiar to the abstract.

Using the melodic kernel as scaffolding, Armstrong builds a more elaborate structure in the last three phrases. The fifth and sixth phrases recall all the elements of the fourth phrase, not just the melodic kernel (example 2.9). The fourth phrase provides a skeleton; the fifth and

EXAMPLE 2.7   Louis Armstrong and His Hot Five, "Big Butter and Egg Man," 16 November 1926, Louis Armstrong's paraphrase of the original melody (mm. 1–16).

EXAMPLE 2.8   Louis Armstrong and His Hot Five, "Big Butter and Egg Man," 16
November 1926: a) three backward and three forward phrases in Louis Armstrong's solo;
b) melodic kernel at return of A (m. 25).

sixth phrases each add an anacrusis; the fifth elaborates the second
half; and the sixth elaborates the first half. The endings of the last two
phrases clearly echo the ending of the fourth phrase. The B♭–G ending
elaborates the fourth phrase by descending a whole step and repeating
the figure, and the A–C ending resolves or answers both previous endings. We have already seen how it complements the fifth phrase ending.
The rising A–C resolves the fourth phrase ending even more strongly,
by exactly inverting it. Admittedly, the sense of resolution here must
be viewed as an idiosyncratic one not based especially on tonal relationships. But I do perceive a sense of closure at the end of the sixth
phrase that seems not only to address the ends of the fourth and fifth
phrases but in some way to complete them. One might compare the

three phrase endings to two half-cadences followed by a full cadence in classical music.

Still another parsing of the music reveals correspondences every other measure. Due to the constancy of pitch (A), the beginnings of mm. 1, 3, and 5 sound like rhythmic experiments that Armstrong alternately discards for the eighth-note/dotted quarter figure at m. 7 (example 2.10). The first experiment presents the simplest combination: three quarter notes. The second retains the downbeat on three and introduces the dotted quarter on the upbeat of one. The third retains the dotted quarter on the upbeat of one and brings back the downbeat on one. And the fourth combines elements of the three preceding experiments by retaining both downbeats on one and three and the dotted quarter on the upbeat of one. The resulting eighth-note/dotted quarter figure is thus the answer to Armstrong's question, which, figuratively, might be: What rhythm should I use? As if finally satisfied with this figure, he thereafter presents it at the beginning of the other odd measures (example 2.11). One variation of the rhythm at m. 11 (which recalls m. 3) saves the pattern from sounding mechanical. Otherwise, the figure (also its precursors in mm. 1, 3, and 5) supplies structural coherence, dividing the passage into two-bar segments.[31]

To summarize, in the first half of "Big Butter" Armstrong creates a rich network of melodic relationships, inviting us to consider the music from various angles: as four groups of two-bar phrases followed by two groups of four; as two groups of three unequal phrases; and as eight groups of two-bar phrases. The phrases interact like the lines of a particularly complex poetry, calling back and forth multifarious "rhymes"

31 See also Schuller, *Early Jazz*, 104.

EXAMPLE 2.10   "Big Butter and Egg Man," rhythmic experiments in four phrases.

EXAMPLE 2.11   Louis Armstrong and His Hot Five, "Big Butter and Egg Man," 16 November 1926, eighth-note/dotted quarter rhythm and its variants in odd measures of solo.

which vary in strength and structural prominence. The complexity of the rhyme scheme creates a mood of constant surprise, keeping the listener off-balance. Yet Armstrong takes care to complete unfinished business, tying together loose ends and bringing the passage to a satisfying conclusion. Armstrong paraphrases aspects of the melody en route, but he also riffs repeatedly on a single melodic fragment. Every musical event recalls a preceding one, and several possess multiple meanings. Although Armstrong's variational technique may seem extravagant, no gestures are superfluous; all have a demonstrable origin and purpose.

The bridge (C section) of the solo transposes the melodic kernel at higher pitch levels than the AB section, thereby continuing the thread of coherence but with greater energy. The first phrase of the bridge presents the kernel a fourth higher and the second phrase a whole step higher than the original (example 2.12). Yet the second phrase doesn't complete the kernel; it ends on A rather than the melody note G that Armstrong played in the opening ensemble. The resulting dissonance, which Armstrong emphasizes by repeating the A, creates a tension that is broken by the final figure of the bridge, which Schuller justifiably calls "the high point of the solo."[32] Schuller and Hodeir admire this phrase for its hard-driving rhythmic swing more characteristic of later jazz eras than the 1920s. Structurally, however, the phrase marks the strongest point because of its recapitulatory nature: it represents a compact variation of the final phrase of the AB section and, as we have seen, the clearest, most concise statement of the melodic kernel (example 2.13).

EXAMPLE 2.12   Louis Armstrong and His Hot Five, "Big Butter and Egg Man," 16 November 1926, presentation of melodic kernel in bridge.

_____
32 Schuller, *Early Jazz*, 105.

EXAMPLE 2.13   Louis Armstrong and His Hot Five, "Big Butter and Egg Man," 16 November 1926, variation at the end of the bridge of final phrase of AB section.

A GIFT FROM RHYTHM TAP?

Taken together, the many nuanced correspondences in "Big Butter" mark a wide departure from Armstrong's earlier practice, with its blunt modules and variational routines. What could have provoked such a dramatic change in style? In an interview from 1970, tenor saxophonist Bud Freeman proposed one theory. He recalled that the Sunset Café

> had a floor show—for which Louie, as a member of the band, had to play—*and this I think was responsible for a change in his style.…*He was now playing trumpet, working with acts like Brown and McGraw, a fabulous dance team; Rector and Cooper, another pair of great dancers—and when Buck and Bubbles would play the Palace downtown, they would come in and double at the Sunset.[33]

Freeman hints that the primary change came in the form of Armstrong's upper-register playing, and it may well be that the dynamic leaps and high kicks of the Sunset dancers inspired Armstrong to reach upward as well. But it seems just as likely that the dancers stimulated a new rhythmic flexibility, especially in view of Armstrong's unusually close onstage relationship with Brown and McGraw, a husband-and-wife dance team from New Orleans.

After achieving success in vaudeville and prominent cabarets like the Cotton Club in Harlem, Herbert Brown (1899–1944) and Naomi McGraw (1901–68) began a lengthy stint at the Sunset Café in June 1926.[34] They

33 Bud Freeman, in conversation with Irving Kolodin, "The Father and His Flock," *Saturday Review,* 4 July 1970, 16.

34 For a fuller account of Armstrong's work with Brown and McGraw, see Brian Harker, "Louis Armstrong, Eccentric Dance, and the Evolution of Jazz on the Eve of Swing," *Journal of the American Musicological Society* 61 (2008): 67–121.

were known for a supremely energetic tap dancing style, one that mingled fast, intricate steps with acrobatic leaps and Lindy hopping aerials. They were, in short, exponents of *rhythm tap*, a new type of tap dancing distinguished from the traditional style mostly for its greater physical demands and rhythmic complexity. Sometime in the summer or fall Brown and McGraw teamed up with Armstrong to perform joint routines during Percy Venable's floor shows. As Doc Cheatham put it,

> There was an act called Brown and McGraw, jazz dancers. That Louis Armstrong made…this couple famous, cause he played every step they made. And he screamed the whole act, playing trumpet, and every movement that they made, Louis would make it on his horn, and that made Brown and McGraw one of the most famous dance acts in Chicago, at that time….Louie Armstrong was the *first* one to play that act….So, after that, when [Brown and McGraw] went out [on tour] without Louie they had to have a trumpet player that could play….They had everything written out….So you had to go on the stage and play with them.[35]

Armstrong explained the collaboration in similar terms: "There was the team of Brown and McGraw. They did a jazz dance that just wouldn't quit. I'd blow for their act, and every step they made, I put the notes to it. They liked the idea so well they had it arranged."[36]

Two important points stand out in these accounts: first, Armstrong evidently played the dancers' rhythms, not the other way around; and second, the routines became fixed, to the point that Armstrong's lines were eventually notated in an arrangement. Both of these points make sense when applied to "Big Butter and Egg Man," a solo that suggests a new approach to rhythm, and one, also, that probably became a fixed composition over time. "Big Butter" is one of the few numbers on which we know, thanks to Earl Hines's testimony, that Brown and McGraw performed,[37] and Armstrong recorded it in November 1926, at the height of his involvement with the dancers. In view of these facts, it seems plausible that the rich motivic integration in "Big Butter" may reflect, in part, the innovations of rhythm tap, and Armstrong's absorption of them through his interaction with Brown and McGraw.

35 Jazz Oral History Project, Cheatham interview.
36 Shapiro and Hentoff, *Hear Me Talkin' to Ya*, 106.
37 Dance, *Earl Hines*, 49.

Returning to the music, Armstrong's solo possesses anomalous features that might be explained by a dancer's influence. This is especially true of the bridge, which Schuller calls "the imaginative climax of the solo" (example 2.5a).[38] The second half of the bridge contains the most characteristically taplike rhythmic sequence and the closest thing we have to a smoking gun. The lengthy succession of eighth-quarter-eighth figures (mm. 20–22), though atypical for Armstrong and other jazz soloists from this time, was a standard combination among tap dancers.[39] As we shall see, Bill "Bojangles" Robinson featured it prominently in his famous "Stair Dance" routine. The opening of the bridge (mm. 16–17) contains allusions to tap as well, but here the connection is more subtle. Although the melody is unremarkable, in other ways Armstrong had never played anything like it—at least not on record. By themselves, the two kinds of triplets are not unusual. But his use of them here—two sets of eighth-note triplets followed in augmentation by two sets of quarter-note triplets—has the flashy rhythmic character of an exciting tap routine at its peak.

More intriguingly, Armstrong animates those opening eighth-note triplets with rapid alternations between standard and false fingering. Such a *bariolage*-like effect would later become commonplace among jazz trumpet and saxophone players, but at this time it was still rarely used.[40] White cornetist Red Nichols claimed to have shown Armstrong how to use false fingering in 1924–25, when the two of them played for opposing bands at the Roseland Ballroom (Armstrong for Henderson, and Nichols for Sam Lanin).[41] Armstrong tossed off a brief false fingering effect during the second chorus of "Cornet Chop Suey" (first break), but this moment in the middle of "Big Butter" represents his first prominent use of the device. Perhaps he was trying to emulate a tap dancing effect. A classical trumpet player might have used double- or triple-tonguing, but Armstrong did not have the training to execute these techniques. Multiple tonguing, in any case, aimed to eliminate tiny differences of pitch and timbre; Armstrong's solution magnified those differences every time

---

38 Schuller, *Early Jazz*, 105.

39 The freshness of this fairly simple rhythmic sequence in a jazz solo from this time is suggested by Schuller, a stern critic of cliché, who characterized it enthusiastically as "a superbly syncopated" line. *Early Jazz*, 105.

40 For a discussion of this technique in the playing of early saxophonists Jimmy Dorsey and Lester Young, see Lewis Porter, *Lester Young*, rev. ed. (Ann Arbor: University of Michigan Press, 2005), 50–53.

41 Teachout, *Pops*, 84.

he changed fingerings, thereby matching more closely the uneven rippling effect of a tap dancer alternating rapidly between left and right or heel and toe. False fingering enabled Armstrong to create the effect of fast articulation while remaining (essentially) on a single pitch, just like the pitch of the taps.

Another anomaly appears at the beginning of the solo (mm. 1–6). The leisurely unfolding of Armstrong's thrice-stated question is unusual, especially the three full beats of rest that separate each entry. That's a lot of empty space for an Armstrong solo from this period—especially a hot solo in medium tempo. Earlier in this chapter, I portrayed this passage rhetorically as three calls in search of a response. Imagining the piece as it was performed each night at the Sunset, however, one might consider a more conventional call-and-response sequence, with Armstrong's calls answered each time with a flurry of taps by Brown and McGraw. If Armstrong and the dancers performed together on this piece, it is unthinkable that Brown and McGraw would remain still and silent during these openings. The dance fills would help make sense of a long-mysterious passage.

The sudden shift in Armstrong's rhythmic practices makes sense when we compare them with combinations favored by early tap dancers. Consider, first of all, the beginning of Bill "Bojangles" Robinson's signature "Stair Dance," performed to the music of "Old Folks at Home" and filmed in 1932 (example 2.14).[42] The most famous black tap dancer of his day, Robinson by this time was fifty-four years old, a representative of the old school. In contrast to the young rhythm tappers, Robinson perfected old steps rather than creating new ones.[43] Not surprisingly, the rhythms of his "Stair Dance" consist of the same ragtime patterns we encountered in Armstrong's early solos, but in an even purer form. The cakewalk rhythm (mm. 1, 3, 6) alternates with secondary rag (mm. 2, 4, 7–8), which then alternates with straight quarter notes (mm. 9–16) and even the Oliver rhythm (mm. 17–20). This is not to say that Robinson had no relevance for the rising generation. Both as a symbol of commercial success and as an exemplar of flawless execution, Robinson inspired young dancers, and his "Stair Dance" (though deemed "not difficult" by Eddie Rector, one of Brown and McGraw's fellow entertainers

---

42 This short film is included in the video anthology *At the Jazz Band Ball: Early Hot Jazz, Song, and Dance*, produced by Sherwin Dunner and Richard Nevins, 60 min., Yazoo Video, © 2000, videocassette.

43 Marshall Stearns and Jean Stearns, *Jazz Dance: The Story of American Vernacular Dance* (New York: Macmillan, 1968; reprint, New York: Da Capo, 1994), 187.

EXAMPLE 2.14 Rhythms to Bill "Bojangles" Robinson's "Stair Dance," performed to the music of "Old Folks at Home" (1932).

at the Sunset) was widely imitated.[44] Perhaps that is why the repeated eighth-quarter-eighth rhythms in the second four-bar phrase (mm. 5–6) also appear in "Big Butter and Egg Man" (mm. 20–22): Armstrong was simply following the steps Brown and McGraw had learned from Robinson or his disciples. In most respects, however, Robinson's rhythmic language seems a far cry from that of "Big Butter."

By contrast, the Nicholas Brothers' performance on "China Boy," also filmed in 1932, shows a remarkable kinship to Armstrong's new rhythmic style (example 2.15).[45] Whereas Robinson "was a *Buck* dancer who didn't change his style in sixty years," according to one contemporary,[46] Fayard and Harold Nicholas, aged eighteen and eleven in the film, represented the latest trends in rhythm tap. A glance at the transcription shows the enormous difference in conception: contrasts abound not only between but within measures (particularly in the steps of the more experienced Fayard), and lengthy patterns are traded for shorter rhythms that change frequently, sometimes from one beat to the next. The tempo, much slower than the "Stair Dance," allows the brothers to display their complex figures, just as "Big Butter" (likewise slower than "Cake Walking Babies") opened things up for Armstrong. The complexity on "China Boy" obviously exceeds that of "Big Butter," but this might be explained by the rapid evolution of rhythm tap during the six-year gap separating the two performances. The more important point is the principle of constant variability so dear to the heart of the rhythm tappers—and, post–"Big Butter," to Armstrong as well. This principle became a fetish to ambitious dancers such as Charles "Honi" Coles, a youngster in Philadelphia in the late 1920s who took pride in being able to tap "six, seven, and sometimes eight full choruses of a thirty-two-bar tune without repeating a step."[47]

The evidence is circumstantial. But taken together, it suggests a reasonable hypothesis: as Armstrong followed the elaborate combinations of dance steps performed by Brown and McGraw on "Big Butter," the exchanges between them suggested new possibilities for other tunes as well, forcing Armstrong out of his habitual lines of thought and into new rhythmic sequences. As dancers known for their difficult steps, Brown

44 Stearns and Stearns, *Jazz Dance*, 185, 187.
45 This performance, accompanied by Eubie Blake and His Orchestra, was part of the Vitaphone movie short *Pie, Pie, Blackbird*, which has been included as an extra on the reissue of the 1929 film *Hallelujah*, directed by King Vidor, 100 min., Warner Brothers Home Video, 2006, DVD.
46 Stearns and Stearns, *Jazz Dance*, 187.
47 Stearns and Stearns, *Jazz Dance*, 306.

EXAMPLE 2.15   Rhythms to the Nicholas Brothers' tap routine on "China Boy," accompanied by Eubie Blake and His Orchestra (1932).

and McGraw in some sense imposed on him a new world of corporeal rhythms unfamiliar from the playing of his fellow musicians. Armstrong's attempt to duplicate details of their extraordinary maneuvers crystallized a new rhythmic strategy, breaking the impasse posed by formulaic thinking, fracturing his patterns into smaller pieces, and reconstituting his style.

Whatever the impetus for change, "Big Butter and Egg Man" marked a turning point in the Hot Five series. In later solos such as "Potato Head Blues," "Struttin' with Some Barbecue," "Hotter Than That," "Weatherbird," and "Muggles," we hear a similar rhetorical fluidity, with few of the constraints that bedeviled Armstrong in such early recordings as "Cake Walking Babies." In these mature solos he employs a rhythmic vocabulary that is free, flexible, and endlessly inventive. This vocabulary became the foundation for swing, the new jazz language of the 1930s. Just as important, Armstrong demonstrated how to knit this variable language together, how to tell a story that would make sense to a wide range of listeners. In this way, "Big Butter and Egg Man" became a rhetorical model for jazz of the future.

CHAPTER 3

PLAYING THE CHANGES
"POTATO HEAD BLUES"

(10 MAY 1927)

> I started to go through all that business of studying them big
> chords and harmonies way back, but then I found out I'd been
> playing them all the time.
>
> —LOUIS ARMSTRONG

NOTWITHSTANDING THE MAJOR RHETORICAL advance represented by "Big Butter and Egg Man," there remained an important additional step to be taken along the path from the two-bar break of the ragtime age to the full-length solo of the swing era. As jazz historians have long known, lengthy solos for the cornet consisted primarily of melodic paraphrases in the early 1920s. It's not that players didn't understand harmony, or how to improvise on chords. But their fundamental conception was focused on varying a melody—either the melody of the tune or one of their own. Improvisation depended on embellishing a routine. For all its structural elegance and internal logic, "Big Butter" was this kind of solo. While paraphrase solos would continue to be played, another approach to improvisation opened a new vision of jazz, launching a true paradigm shift in the 1920s. This approach involved articulating the harmony or the chord progression of the tune being played. Once the focus shifted to the harmony, solos became more abstract and large-scale routines more difficult to sustain. In the place of routines, musicians created long extemporaneous solos, whose contours were harmonically fixed but melodically unpredictable. Free melody made possible the open-ended jam sessions of the 1930s and 1940s and the extended solo recordings of the 1950s. Possibly nothing was more important to the future of jazz as we know it than developing a robust harmonic approach to improvisation.

The funny thing is, while Armstrong played a leading role in this development he also resisted taking full advantage of the new approach. For most of his career he seemed indifferent to its possibilities for creative exploration. Out of loyalty to tradition, apparently, he tended to favor melodic paraphrases or, at most, to play harmony-based solos severely restricted in length or content. Although he was a fierce competitor in cutting contests early on, these battles brought out high-note displays, not clever harmonic interpretations. Nor did Armstrong figure prominently in the jam sessions of the swing era. You would not have found him hanging out on Fifty-second Street after hours, playing chorus after chorus of "What Is This Thing Called Love?" The free-floating framework and prolonged spontaneity of such marathons were essentially alien to Armstrong's conception during this period. Nevertheless, for several years in the 1920s he cultivated both the discipline of playing the changes and the exploratory give-and-take of the jam session (witness his riveting seat-of-the-pants dialogue with Earl Hines on "Weatherbird"). In so doing he laid the groundwork for up-and-coming players, who turned his experimentation into standard practice.

Given Armstrong's desultory commitment to harmonic improvisation, why did he start down this path in the first place? Since to all appearances neither he nor his contemporaries have discussed this matter at length, we can only conjecture. Clearly, he wasn't motivated by any pseudo-modernist impulse, à la Duke Ellington, to advance the language of jazz. Nor was he drawn to the intricacies of harmony, as was his colleague Coleman Hawkins. "I never was one for going on and on about the changes of a tune," he said, "all I want to do is hear that chord."[1] Perhaps, then, it was not the harmonic framework per se that attracted him, but the acrobatic dynamism of arpeggiated playing. Not the intellectual concept of navigating a chord progression, but the vaudevillian idea of playing cartwheels on the trumpet. Not the desire to leave behind the melodic paraphrase, but the urge somehow to perpetuate the excitement of clarinet style in a freer, less derivative form. Once others had embraced

---

1   Jones and Chilton, *Louis*, 240.

this type of playing and the novelty had worn off, Armstrong was free to return to a simpler style, which he did. Perhaps, in his mind, now that playing arpeggios no longer distinguished him from his peers, he could let the younger generation knock themselves out.

For Armstrong, overtly harmonic thinking began with the sawtooth arpeggios of his early experimentation with clarinet style. With Fletcher Henderson he embraced arpeggios not directly associated with the clarinet. During this period he confined arpeggios primarily to the margins of his solos—introductions, breaks, phrase endings, and so forth—while filling the body with melodic paraphrases. This division between melodic paraphrase and arpeggiated break would increasingly dissolve in the years to come. One of his central concerns at the beginning of the Hot Five series was to integrate the two approaches into a unified solo style—in essence, to keep the excitement of the break going throughout. This required him to rely on harmonic progressions far more than he had done in the past. It took a while, though, for Armstrong to create a convincing melody based on the chords of a piece. "Oriental Strut" (1926) is highly arpeggiated, for instance, but also somewhat stilted and predictable. By the time he recorded "Potato Head Blues" a year later, however, the awkwardness was gone. This recording relies even more heavily on broken chords, and yet the solo's inventiveness and fluency mark it as one of his greatest recordings. Here Armstrong shows himself to be a master of the changes, however misleading that may be for the course of his future career.

STRAINING AGAINST THE STRAIN

In the early 1920s jazz musicians felt a special duty toward the melody. This was so in New Orleans, according to drummer Baby Dodds, who insisted that the melody must be heard "at all times."[2] It was equally true in Chicago. In fact, Dave Peyton used the same expression as Dodds to make a similar point in more flowery language: "I love to hear it when the melody is dominant *at all times*, garnished with theoretic harmonic figures and founded on pure basic musical principles." On another occasion, Peyton chided a band for drifting from the melody: "The boys want to be a little careful when they get to jazzing. They are loosening the melody by all trying to jazz 'em at once. The theme should always be audible."[3] In polyphony it was okay to leave the melody if another player

---

2   Brothers, *Louis Armstrong's New Orleans*, 45.
3   *Defender*, 7 August 1926, 6; 28 August 1926, 6.

was carrying it, but abstract improvisation accompanied only by the rhythm section was apparently not okay, according to Peyton.

In keeping with this philosophy, virtually all of Armstrong's solos with Fletcher Henderson paraphrase the melody of the piece being played. His melodic paraphrases range from transparent rephrasing to only distant echoes of the melody. Sometimes he plays the original melody with only minor rhythmic alterations (e.g., "Tell Me, Dreamy Eyes"); other times he adds extensive melodic embellishments and interpolations as well as new rhythms ("Words"). Moving toward greater abstraction, he may create a new melody based on fragments ("Go 'Long, Mule") or even on important pitches ("Copenhagen") of the original melody. In "Copenhagen," Armstrong lifts what might be called in Schenkerian terms the "structural" pitches from the clarinet trio played earlier, and in a sort of "composing out" process, elaborates his own melody on the foundation thus laid. Here it seems that behind his solo statement Armstrong is no longer hearing the entire original melody (as seems evident in, say, "Tell Me, Dreamy Eyes") but rather a skeletal version that suggests global contours for his solo but nothing more.

Improvisation brought incremental changes to Armstrong's melodic routines that sometimes led him to think harmonically. Close similarities among alternate takes reveal Armstrong's improvisational method: to tinker with already stable designs (whether a commercial melody or one of his own) rather than to start fresh with each new performance. In the course of tinkering, Armstrong often pressed the borders of his melodic vehicles, as if trying to find a freer mode of expression. On at least one occasion, he moved so far from the original melody that by the last take he was essentially playing on the harmony.

In January 1925 Armstrong recorded four takes of "Why Couldn't It Be Poor Little Me?"[4] Armstrong's solo in the first take loosely paraphrases the opening melody, primarily by coinciding with the pitches on the first beat of mm. 1, 3, and 5 (example 3.1). After that Armstrong abandons the melody until the last half of the solo, when he matches the first pitches of each measure again. The next three takes, recorded during a single session later in the month,[5] show still greater independence from the melody. At first glance the second take might seem almost totally unrelated,

---

4   Henderson recorded six takes of "Why Couldn't It Be Poor Little Me?" (matrix number 5811), of which the first and third were never released. For the sake of clarity, I refer to takes 2, 4, 5, and 6 as the first, second, third, and fourth (issued) takes in the following discussion.

5   Jos Willems, *All of Me: The Complete Discography of Louis Armstrong*, Studies in Jazz, No. 51 (Lanham, MD: Scarecrow Press, 2006), 21–22.

but actually the first three and a half measures of the solo represent an ornamented expansion of the melody's opening figure (example 3.2). While the third take largely repeats the expansion, the fourth is modified just enough to sever this fragile link with the original melody. From this point on, the solo in takes 2, 3, and 4 repeatedly elaborates a blues figure around the lowered third. One point, however, merits attention: in m. 7 Armstrong experiments with various forms of the F major triad, showing an effort to replace melodic thinking with ideas based specifically on the harmony.

Why do the second, third, and fourth takes of "Why Couldn't It Be Poor Little Me?" connect less strongly to the original melody than the first does? Whereas the first and second takes vaguely paraphrase the melody in their own ways, the third and fourth paraphrase the *paraphrase* of the

EXAMPLE 3.1   Fletcher Henderson and His Orchestra, "Why Couldn't It Be Poor Little Me?," mid-January 1925, melody and Louis Armstrong's four solos (first half).

second take, thereby drifting progressively farther away from the melodic source.[6] For this reason, the first take differs strongly from the other three, which are, in turn, very similar to one another. By the second recording session Armstrong had rethought his approach to the solo and fashioned each take according to his new ideas.

Even so, an evolutionary thread connects all four takes. Immediately after the opening (m. 2), take 2 elaborates material beginning two beats earlier in take 1, which takes 3 and 4 then elaborate in turn. The genealogy becomes especially clear in mm. 6–7. Take 4, with its blues inflections, might bear little resemblance to take 1 in m. 6, but takes 2 and 3 provide a link to show the descent. And the next measure confirms the relationships beyond doubt. The first two takes each present variations on the F major triad: a descending arpeggio in take 1 and an ascending chromatic triplet in take 2. Take 3 returns to the descending arpeggio, but take 4 combines the two ideas, unifying all four solos. Such examples prove that while Armstrong had moved to a different level of thinking by the second recording session, he continued to develop ideas from the first. This developmental thinking led him directly into a more abstract, harmonic way of playing.

THE ILLUSION OF MOVEMENT

In addition to the positive force of incremental improvisation, the negative force of stock embellishments may have nudged Armstrong toward a harmonic conception. Thomas Brothers makes the insightful observation

6   Jeffrey Magee speculates in a similar vein: "It seems unlikely that the music [for Armstrong's solos] was actually written down. More likely, Armstrong's encounter with a new melody caused him to recompose the tune (on trumpet) and use his revision as the basis for later solos. From this perspective, Armstrong's approach resembled that of a traditional composer more than of a band musician who renders his part the same way each time." Jeffrey Magee, "The Music of Fletcher Henderson and His Orchestra in the 1920s" (PhD diss., University of Michigan, 1992), 327.

that in his melodic paraphrase solos, Armstrong combined the functions of playing lead and second, capturing "the vigor and richness of collective improvisation in a single line."[7] That's a good way of thinking about it, particularly with respect to his solos with Henderson. In paraphrasing a melody, Armstrong aimed for a sort of bustling turbulence that created the illusion of movement, if not always forward motion.

This aim led to a reliance on stock figures, some of which were introduced in chapter 2. For Armstrong's harmonic development, the most important of these were the oscillating seconds, thirds, and fourths that we encountered in "Go 'Long Mule" and "Cake Walking Babies." These rocking figures function a bit like the Alberti bass did in music of the classic period: they animate the texture, creating a lively surface, but do little to advance the argument of the music. Unlike the Alberti bass, of course, Armstrong's rocking figures appear only briefly amid more meaningful gestures. Still, their appearance often seems to suggest a momentary lapse of inspiration or inventiveness. Or to put it more accurately (and fairly), perhaps they indicate that Armstrong was reaching for a fullness of meaningful animated expression that didn't yet exist in jazz, even in his own fecund melodic vocabulary. The oscillating thirds and fourths seem especially to symbolize a yearning for more complete harmonic elucidation, as if the figures simply needed to cook a bit longer before attaining their destiny as full-blown triads and seventh chords.

Because stock figures decrease significantly around the same time that Armstrong begins playing explicitly on chord progressions, it seems possible that the tedium of formulas helped push him toward harmonic improvisation just as it led him to search for new rhythms. Maybe he wearied of the static rocking figures and wanted to find dynamic motives that actually led somewhere. Or maybe he just got tired of playing jumpy versions of other people's melodies and decided to play his own melodies that jumped naturally.

EXPERIMENTING WITH ARPEGGIOS

"I never have liked a wrong harmony," Armstrong once said,

> Going right back to my earliest days singing in the quartet, as a kid it just came natural. I started to go through all that business of studying them big chords and harmonies way back, but then I found out I'd been playing them all the time. To me, [studying harmony] was like

---

7   Brothers, *Louis Armstrong's New Orleans*, 291.

the idea of learning to say a greeting in each country I visit. Man, with all that studying and thinking about what's going to come next I'd end up saying pleased to meet you in German when I got off the plane in Italy. When I say "Good Evening Everybody," they know I *mean* it- same with the music, just do what come natural.[8]

In the middle of this paean to intuitive playing, Armstrong makes the fascinating admission that at one time he had set out to understand harmony in the formal sense of learning chord names, spellings, and perhaps even functions. Southern jazz musicians who came North without much formal musical training often tried to remedy their deficiencies by reading manuals, taking lessons or correspondence courses, and practicing excerpts from Western classical literature. A classical foundation added to a player's sense of class and, sometimes, his earning power. Dave Peyton praised Bob Shoffner and Luis Russell, two New Orleans musicians playing with King Oliver, for studying music theory: "These young men play all night in Chicago and are making the sacrifice of sleep by getting up early twice a week to take their lessons." Such diligence would help guard against "discordant playing," in which "so-called jazz artists... [ruin] the composition by injecting figures that have no relation to the basic harmonic setting." "To improvise requires art in the player," said Peyton. "He should be acquainted with counterpoint and harmony."[9]

Peyton often railed against "discordant playing" in jazz, which may have been more widespread in the 1920s than we know. A strain of proud know-nothingism had typified some jazz practitioners ever since 1917, when the Original Dixieland Jazz Band boasted of their musical illiteracy to buttress their credentials as authentic novelty artists.[10] It stands to reason that one way to demonstrate such ignorance (whether real or feigned) would be to play at odds with the chord progression. To do so may have seemed the appropriate harmonic counterpart to the structural incoherence mandated by vaudevillian aesthetics. In 1927 one commentator for *The Etude* seized upon this practice as evidence of jazz's inherent weakness outside the "symphonic" realm:

8 Jones and Chilton, *Louis*, 240–41.
9 *Defender*, 29 January 1927, 6; 3 July 1926, 6.
10 ODJB cornetist Nick LaRocca famously said: "I don't know how many pianists we tried before we found one who couldn't read music." Frederick Ramsey Jr. and Charles Edward Smith, eds., *Jazzmen* (New York: Harcourt Brace, 1939; reprint, New York: Limelight, 1985), 51. For more on such "calculated primitivism" in early jazz, see William Howland Kenney, *Chicago Jazz: A Cultural History, 1904–1930* (New York: Oxford University Press, 1993), 41–42.

A short time ago a celebrated (or shall we say notorious) Jazzaphonist explained to the writer how some of the "weird" effects were produced in Jazz. You simply played the same melody on one instrument a half tone higher than the other instruments in the group. Simple! What better recipe could there be for Cacophony. Lacking the genius of Gershwin and others who have employed jazz as a ladder to climb to greater heights, the improvising Jazzaphonist deliberately makes all kinds of musical grammatical blunders under the misconception that he is doing something particularly smart. Just now the public is waking up to all this claptrap and is beginning to realize that it is largely a waste of time to expect unusual results from people who make a brag of being illiterate.[11]

The author of this opinion was certainly white, as was, probably, his corresponding "Jazzaphonist." But judging from the frequency of Peyton's complaints, it appears likely that a fair amount of "discordant playing" took place on the South Side as well. Peyton may have felt compelled to wage a campaign not only against uneducated musicians but also against literate anarchists, the kind of soloists who would deliberately play a half-step away from the proper key. Armstrong, who never liked a "wrong harmony," would have agreed with Peyton on this point. His decision to study harmony should be understood against this backdrop of know-nothingism and nihilism among some jazz musicians of the time.

When might this learning have taken place? We know that during his time on the riverboats, around 1919–21, Armstrong was still working on the fundamentals of sight-reading.[12] Looking ahead, by 1927 he had apparently become at least somewhat familiar with standard chord notation, for in that year he published his jazz manuals, *50 Hot Choruses* and *125 Hot Breaks*, with Melrose Music. To produce these books, pianist Elmer Schoebel explained, Armstrong simply played fifty-three solo choruses and 125 breaks, which were recorded onto wax cylinders. Schoebel transcribed the lines, gave the notation to Melrose, and the books were published.[13] To play the choruses, Armstrong could have relied on his knowledge of the tunes, all of which were well-known New Orleans-style compositions like "High Society" and "Tin Roof Blues." But the breaks in the book are only labeled by key, chord, and chord quality. Armstrong plays in every key around the circle of fifths, including three

11 *The Etude* (April 1927): 255.
12 Harker, "Early Musical Development," 60–63.
13 Elmer Schoebel and Herman Openneer Jr., "The Elmer Schoebel Story," *Doctor Jazz* 32 (October 1968): 6–7.

or four breaks each for three chord types—major, minor, and dominant seventh—in the more common keys. He also plays three breaks for each of the three fully diminished seventh chords. Although he was probably accompanied by a piano during the recording (the breaks are all preceded by a piano chord in the book), it seems likely that he knew the chords theoretically as well as aurally. Some of the breaks, after all, are more inspired than others, and some come across as a perfunctory running of the triad, as though he were thinking too theoretically—as though, to recall Armstrong's own comparison, he were straining to speak German instead of letting it come naturally. In any case, by 1927 Armstrong had probably learned his chords fairly well, as his outstanding harmonic improvisations of this year suggest.

Sometime between 1922 and 1927, then, Armstrong must have worked to learn harmony, probably under Lil's tutelage. Such a regimen would have been in keeping with her grand plans for him. A well-qualified classical teacher, Hardin herself studied at the Chicago College of Music, earning her teacher's certificate in 1928.[14] We know that she drilled Armstrong in classical literature at the baby grand piano in their home; one can imagine her giving harmony lessons as well. Early efforts to play chordally suggest that he was, in fact, trying out new skills, with sometimes awkward results. As his Henderson solos indicate, two-bar breaks posed little challenge, probably because he worked them out in advance. But he seems less confident in stop-time passages, which were often longer than breaks but shorter than full-length solos. In the stop-time passage near the end of his solo on "Cake Walking Babies," Armstrong simply plugs the notes of the requisite harmony, an $E\flat^7$ chord, into a stock rhythmic sequence, two-note secondary rag (example 3.3). The bland rhythm calls attention to his equally dutiful approach to harmony. This is no timeless Armstrong melody, but a successful navigation of a dominant seventh chord at a brisk tempo, nothing more. Similarly, in his recording of "Cornet Chop Suey" (but not the copyright deposit), Armstrong fills two stop-time passages with figures that run up and down the chords a bit too methodically, flecked here and there by predictably unpredictable syncopations (example 3.4).

At the beginning of the Hot Five series, Armstrong shows a striking new interest in harmonic playing, in some cases breaking sharply from the paraphrase style he had used with Henderson. During this period he sometimes used his old rocking figures as a bridge to fully arpeggiated

14 *Defender*, 9 June 1928, 6.

EXAMPLE 3.3   Clarence Williams's Blue Five, "Cake Walking Babies (from Home)," 8 January 1925, beginning of Louis Armstrong's stop-time solo.

EXAMPLE 3.4   Louis Armstrong and His Hot Five, "Cornet Chop Suey," 26 February 1926, second chorus, Louis Armstrong's arpeggios in stop-time passages.

playing. "Muskrat Ramble," a tune in march form, may be his first full-length solo not obviously based on a preexisting melody (example 3.5). In mm. 3–4, he does toy with the B♭–A♭–G–F figure from m. 4 of the melody of the B section, and the octave descent in mm. 6–7 roughly follows the original tune. But the rest of the solo bears little relation to the melody, having a form and logic all its own. He relies on stock figures, both rhythmic and melodic, to get the solo started. With the exception of the Oliver rhythm in the first measure of the section, the opening depends almost entirely on two-note secondary rag (mm. 0–5). Likewise, the melody is based on oscillating seconds (m. 0) and thirds (mm. 2–3, 4–5). The rip to A♭ above the staff, however, shows that he is trying, at least, to make his rocking thirds relevant to the underlying chord movement (E♭⁷–A♭), rather than simply using them to fill space, as he often did with Henderson.

We see a similar process in "Oriental Strut," a melodic paraphrase solo recorded on the same day. Armstrong connects each melody note with wide-ranging arpeggios, as if wanting to spread his wings harmonically but fearful of leaving the structural security of the melody (example 3.6). Stock figures again appear prominently. Two-note secondary rag provides much of the rhythmic basis in the first half (mm. 1, 3–4, 6, 8, 15–16). And as in "Muskrat Ramble," Armstrong uses rocking thirds as his entrée into more genuinely chordal playing: the oscillating A–C motive (mm. 1–2) leads directly to an outline of the D♭ triad (mm. 3–4).

EXAMPLE 3.5 Louis Armstrong and His Hot Five, "Muskrat Ramble," 26 February 1926, B section, melody and Louis Armstrong's solo.

Another example occurs at the end of the second A section, where Armstrong plays a distinctive figure with two-note repetitions on the upbeats (m. 23). This figure extends a line of thinking in evidence more than a year earlier, in a solo he played with Fletcher Henderson on "Naughty Man" (first take). In the latter solo Armstrong plays a figure based on

EXAMPLE 3.6   Louis Armstrong and His Hot Five, "Oriental Strut," 26 February 1926, melody and Louis Armstrong's solo.

the same two-note principle, but in the context of rocking (enharmonic) thirds (example 3.7). The progression of this figure from rocking thirds in "Naughty Man" to a complete triad in "Oriental Strut" a year later suggests that his early oscillating figures may indeed have led the way to harmony-based improvisation.

On "Oriental Strut," one cannot help but notice Armstrong's dull repetitions of the chord tones over the D-flat triad (mm. 3–4). He seems paralyzed in part by his unfamiliarity with harmonic playing and in part by his residual obligation to the melody, for the notes he repeats so mechanically are in fact the melody notes. Elsewhere, and particularly on the familiar F major triad (mm. 5–6, 17–18, 21–22), Armstrong moves more fluidly, but here we see the same problem in a different form: instead of repeating chord tones, Armstrong simply runs up and down the harmony, much as he did on the stop-time passages mentioned above. By attaching arpeggios to certain goal notes, he seems as yet unsure how to merge his two instincts for chord-derived and tune-based melody.

"POTATO HEAD BLUES"

All that had changed by the spring of 1927, when Armstrong entered the recording studio with a Hot Five expanded by two—a tubist and a drummer—to form his Hot Seven. Over six sessions held May 7–14, Armstrong made an outstanding batch of recordings with this band: "Willie the Weeper," "Wild Man Blues," "Chicago Breakdown," "Alligator Crawl," "Potato Head Blues," "Melancholy Blues," "Weary Blues," "Twelfth Street Rag," "Keyhole Blues," "S.O.L. Blues," "Gully Low Blues," and "That's When I'll Come Back to You." Many arpeggiated solos in this group work well, including the preacherly ruminations on "Wild Man Blues" and the spectacular cascading descents on "S.O.L. Blues" (discussed in chapter 4). But the jewel in the crown of Armstrong's Hot Seven recordings, at least in terms of harmonic improvisation, is

EXAMPLE 3.8 Louis Armstrong and His Hot Seven, "Potato Head Blues," 10 May 1927, melody and Louis Armstrong's stop-time solo.

* alternate fingerings (B♭ trumpet key)

his famous (full-length) stop-time solo on "Potato Head Blues," a tune in ABAC song form. On this solo, Armstrong makes passing reference to the melody, most strongly at the beginning (mm. 1–3), middle (mm. 17–20), and end (mm. 29–30) (example 3.8). Otherwise he follows his own muse, treating virtually every phrase in arpeggiated fashion. Largely unfettered by pre-determined contours, he constructs melodies around arpeggios rather than vice versa, as on "Oriental Strut."

One measure of the maturity of Armstrong's harmonic thinking lies in the remarkable integrity of this solo. Although one phrase (mm. 15–16) appeared first in his solo on "Tears," the solo manifests a strong melodic coherence at both high and low levels of structure. The solo unfolds in pairs of phrases (like the rhyming couplets of "Tears"), most of which exhibit a call-and-response relationship in which the second phrase recalls elements from the first. This relationship is especially clear in the two phrases that begin the solo: Armstrong augments in mm. 3–4 the short-short-long rhythm from m. 2; the D–D octave descent in mm. 3–4 inverts the F–F ascent in m. 1; and the oscillating A–C motive that opens the first phrase returns at the end of the second. Armstrong creates large-scale coherence in a number of ways. At A prime, the beginning of the second sixteen measures, he recalls the opening of the solo, especially in m. 19, which reiterates the emphasis on D in mm. 2–3, and in m. 20, which nearly duplicates the melodic content of m. 4. Yet the dominance of F over D in m. 19 suggests a registral expansion that, indeed, continues throughout the second half of the solo. Armstrong, in fact, builds a climactic series of three descending arpeggios, shown in brackets in example 3.8. The ledger-line A that begins the first descent reappears much more emphatically exactly four measures later, with an introductory "rip," lengthened duration, and lip shake. After the second descent Armstrong breaks the pattern by waiting two extra measures and by staying well within the lower register. This creates a suspense that makes the final rip to high C (D on the trumpet) and the arpeggiated two-octave descent in mm. 31–32 much more dramatic. The last three measures—by reviving the oscillating A–C motive, and by following an F major arpeggio with a sustained D—also recall the first three, thus rounding off the solo.

Note, too, that while the A–C motive might appear to show Armstrong trotting out his old crutch, the rocking third, he uses it here in a completely motivated way, rather than as a stalling tactic, by connecting it to other events. In doing so he transforms an old stock figure into fodder for invention. Rhythmically, we see a similar freedom. True, Armstrong plays the Oliver rhythm a lot (five times, including variants). But otherwise—for the remaining 85 percent of the solo—his rhythms flow in an effortless stream of fresh and unhackneyed combinations. As in "Big Butter and Egg Man," rhythmic repetitions tend to appear as short patterns folded into larger gestures. At the beginning of the second half of the chorus, Armstrong introduces a motive consisting of an eighth note followed by a dotted quarter (example 3.9). The motive, which we will call x, appears three times on the downbeat (mm. 17, 18, 20), twice in a different metric position. In the middle of this passage, Armstrong varies x further by presenting it on the upbeat and extending the length of the dotted quarter (m. 19). Another repeating element, a group of four eighth notes (y), adds coherence to the passage. Armstrong creates a pleasing reverse symmetry with this motive, presenting it initially in the second half of the measure, just after x (m. 17), then bringing it back in the *first* half of the measure, just *before* x (m. 20). Just as in "Big Butter and Egg Man," we hear these motives as logical, integral elements within the overall phrase, not as interchangeable units in Armstrong's rhythmic inventory.

In light of these sophisticated structural relationships, compare the arpeggios in "Potato Head Blues" with those of "Cake Walking Babies," "Cornet Chop Suey," and "Oriental Strut." Three qualities made the latter recordings sound mechanical in places:

EXAMPLE 3.9 Louis Armstrong and His Hot Seven, "Potato Head Blues," 10 May 1927, rhythmic repetition at the beginning of the second half of the chorus.

1. Armstrong tended to play "up and down" the chords or to repeat chord tones, taking little care to vary the contour.
2. Armstrong typically adhered strictly to the chord tones, as if following a rule not to violate the harmony.
3. Armstrong's rhythms were predictably unpredictable, mingling running eighth notes with syncopations but avoiding longer or shorter rhythmic values that might divert the flow in new and interesting ways.

That Armstrong repeatedly transgressed these three principles on "Potato Head Blues" suggests one reason for its sense of timeless spontaneity. To perform a thought experiment, consider how much weaker the solo might be if played in accordance with them. Example 3.10 shows the first half of the solo reconstructed in the style of "Cake Walking Babies" or "Oriental Strut." Gone is the rhythmic change-up in mm. 3–4, the harmonic rebellions in mm. 6 and 12, the melodic angularity and stepwise voice leading (C–Db–D–E) of mm. 11–14. The difference from the original is stark and telling (even when taking into account the damage one would inevitably inflict by reconstructing this solo). The point is, in the most pedestrian arpeggiated passages of Armstrong's early recordings, let's face it, he is *not* Armstrong but just an ordinary musician struggling to articulate a harmony. "Potato Head Blues," by contrast, is anything but ordinary. Armstrong's seemingly spontaneous—yet coherent—delivery suggests that he had learned to use arpeggios in an unselfconscious manner as fluent elements of his musical language. The somewhat stiff

EXAMPLE 3.10   "Potato Head Blues," first half of Louis Armstrong's stop-time solo reconstructed in the style of "Cake Walking Babies (from Home)" and "Oriental Strut."

deployment of arpeggios in earlier recordings had given way to unpredictability and invention. Most important, arpeggios became the stuff of melody, the very substance of Armstrong's improvisations. In "Potato Head Blues" Armstrong fuses together the previously separate tuneful and chordal aspects of his melodic approach.

A PHANTOM CLASSIC

We don't know much about the origins or social context of "Potato Head Blues." Unlike "Heebie Jeebies" or "Savoy Blues," this solo is not mentioned in Dave Peyton's columns. And unlike "Cornet Chop Suey" or "Big Butter and Egg Man," it does not appear frequently in the reminiscences of other musicians, including those of Armstrong himself. We don't know whether he played it at the Sunset Café or anywhere else outside the studio. We have no alternate takes, and little sense of history leading up to or away from the recording. There is a copyright deposit, submitted six months after the recording, showing a bare-bones lead sheet in Lil's hand, but—unlike the deposits for "Cornet Chop Suey" and "Savoy Blues"—nothing comparable to Armstrong's solo. For the historian, "Potato Head Blues" is a phantom, assuming a netherworld status all the more perplexing for its reputation among critics as perhaps "the most important 'classic' [Armstrong] solo of 1927."[15]

One wonders if Brown and McGraw danced to Armstrong's solo on "Potato Head Blues" as they did on "Big Butter." We know that they performed with Armstrong at the Sunset between 7 and 21 May, conveniently overlapping the time of the recording on 10 May.[16] The stop-time setting would make sense for a collaboration involving tap dancers. And perhaps Armstrong's stunningly acrobatic figurations represented his attempt to mirror the ecstatic leaps and spins of Brown and McGraw around the stage of the Sunset. If so, it would mean that, as with "Big Butter," Armstrong worked out the solo in advance, or at least perfected it over time.

For that matter, premeditation seems likely whether or not Brown and McGraw provided the impetus. In Armstrong's playing, there appears to be a qualitative difference between solos that are rehearsed (whether on or offstage) and those that are improvised. The rehearsed variety, not surprisingly, have a finished quality that sets them apart: think of "Copenhagen," "Shanghai Shuffle," "Cornet Chop Suey," "Big Butter and Egg Man," "S.O.L.

---

15 Gushee, "The Improvisation of Louis Armstrong," 305.
16 *Defender* (national edition), 7 May 1927, 6–7; 21 May 1927, 7.

Blues," and—as will be argued—"West End Blues." We can presumably gauge Armstrong's true improvisations from alternate takes and, occasionally, a more lumbering style. Certainly he was capable of improvising brilliantly, but spontaneity did not always inspire him. "Cake Walking Babies," an improvised battle with Sidney Bechet, conveys fierce energy but also repetitiveness and cliché. We have no alternate takes for "Oriental Strut," but the tediously repeated notes have no counterpart in Armstrong's composed solos. One must assume that this recording, like many of the early Hot Fives, was tossed off in the studio as a one-time performance. The confident and creative deployment of arpeggios in "Potato Head Blues," by contrast, would seem to reflect deliberation and study, experimentation and refinement, on Armstrong's part.

This brings us back to the issue of harmony, and Armstrong's apparent effort to master chord progressions. However much he may have preferred to "do what come natural" in this regard, he also believed, like any vaudeville professional, in perfecting his routine. From this perspective, it's hard to believe that Armstrong didn't spend hours woodshedding the very demanding discipline of negotiating chord progressions (which does not necessarily equate with improvising). Whether improvised, composed, or something in between, "Potato Head Blues" shows that, as far as playing the changes was concerned, all his hard work had finally paid off.

CHAPTER 4

TOP NOTES
"S.O.L. BLUES"/"GULLY LOW BLUES"
(13-14 MAY 1927)

The trumpet is an instrument full of temptation.

—LOUIS ARMSTRONG

THE IDEA OF A MUSICAL INSTRUMENT INVESTED with demonic powers is not new. The Middle Ages viewed the violin (of its day) as the devil's instrument. In the early nineteenth century, Paganini's astounding virtuosity sparked a rumor that he had made a pact with the devil. The Faustian bargain even found its way into African American culture. According to legend, blues singer Robert Johnson met Satan at a crossroads, where he received otherworldly guitar powers in return for his soul. Armstrong's idea of temptation, to be sure, was a little different. He saw the trumpet not as a transmitter of dark gifts but as a receptacle of desire itself, specifically the desire to play high notes—"top notes," in Armstrong's words—and receive acclaim. Just as Jesus was tempted to jump off the pinnacle of the temple to be upheld by angels in the eyes of all, so likewise was St. Louis tempted to defy gravity, by scaling the heights of his instrument in a similar bid for worldly glory. Unlike Jesus, of course, Armstrong yielded to *his* temptation—again and again and again.

In the late 1920s and early 1930s, Armstrong's lifelong fascination with high notes became an obsession, perhaps an addiction. Stories abound of him playing gushing streams of high Cs—350 in a row, by one account—while admiring musicians stood in the wings counting every one.[1] Over the years he gradually climbed to high F, a note well beyond the capacity of most jazz players of the day. He pushed himself so hard that on more than one occasion his upper lip exploded from the effort, splattering blood down his tuxedo front and sidelining him for weeks or months at a time. This willingness to injure himself betrays more than ordinary ambition. In the trumpet world, high notes represent something like the Nibelung's ring of power, capable of bringing money, fame, and influence, but also of corrupting the player beyond the hope of recovery. Just so, in his single-minded pursuit of the upper register, Armstrong dominated his field at the cost of nearly destroying his career. After an especially gruesome blowout in late 1933, he was forced into a prolonged semiretirement while his lip healed. When he finally resumed his regular performing schedule in 1935, it was with an apparently chastened perspective. Twelve years later he made his statement about temptation during a *Down Beat* roundtable. One wonders if he recognized himself in his pious rebuke of the rising generation: "All the young cats want to kill papa, so they start forcing their tone."[2] Needless to say, he knew something about forcing.

Armstrong's vicious self-punishments make sense when we consider them in the gruelingly competitive context of vaudeville. Weaned on old-school doctrines of novelty, Armstrong recognized that high notes could separate him from the pack and capture the public's attention. By the early 1930s, however, attitudes toward jazz were changing rapidly, and artistic purists attacked old-fashioned appeals to the lowest common denominator. Against such critics, Armstrong's friend Preston Jackson defended him: "The public don't understand jazz music as we musicians do. A diminished seventh don't mean a thing to them, but they go for high notes. After all, the public is paying. If musicians depended on musicians at the box office they would starve to death."[3] When Armstrong played 350 high Cs in a row, mere music was beside the point; his obvious and sole purpose was to demonstrate superhuman strength and endurance, virtues beyond the capacity of ordinary trumpet players. Armstrong's

---

1   Laurence Bergreen, *Louis Armstrong: An Extravagant Life* (New York: Broadway Books, 1997), 361.
2   Robert Walser, ed., *Keeping Time: Readings in Jazz History* (New York: Oxford University Press, 1999), 154.
3   Jackson, "Swinging Cats," 5.

stunt calls to mind the fierce competitions of stage performers vying to be the highest high wire act, or the strongest strong man. A close parallel might be Sandow the Magnificent, who in a famous photo is shown supporting nineteen members of Ziegfeld's Trocadero Company on a platform on his back.[4] By playing 350 high Cs in a row, Armstrong—like Sandow—was presenting himself to the world as a stage artist worthy of top billing, guaranteed to elicit awe.

Like his clarinet-style arpeggios, high notes represented a different kind of novelty, one based on difficulty rather than humor. Armstrong was initially regarded as a stunt player for his ability in the high register. The word most often used to describe him is *freak*. In the late 1920s a *Variety* reporter noted that Armstrong "has a style bordering on the freakish when it comes to hitting top notes on the instrument." Another writer made a similar point, hailing his "freakish, high-registered breaks." "The west coast is going wild over the freak playing of Louis," wrote one reviewer of Armstrong's performances at Sebastian's Cotton Club in Los Angeles, where he became especially well-known for his high notes. Suggesting a physical deformity to match Armstrong's musical freakishness, another joked that perhaps he "had an extra lung."[5] Within a few years, however, such terms as *freak* and *stunt* disappeared as Armstrong's techniques went mainstream through the playing of his many imitators.

Like any serious vaudeville artist, Armstrong trained conscientiously offstage. He carefully observed the fate of his teacher and mentor, King Oliver, who developed pyorrhea of the gums, lost his teeth and embouchure, and faded into obscurity. Mindful of this horrifying example (which played out before his eyes in the mid-1920s), Armstrong took scrupulous care of his teeth and gums.[6] He even became the spokesman for a local dentist in Chicago, according to an unidentified newspaper ad from 1928: "Louis Armstrong—World's Greatest Cornetist Now Featured at [the] SAVOY BALLROOM—says that 'It's a poor man who'll let his teeth rot'—Get your TEETH FIXED."[7] In addition, he heeded popular theories about the benefits of deep breathing on trumpet technique, and worked to increase his lung capacity. In the summers at Lake Michigan, according to Rex Stewart, "Louis outswam almost everybody, doing at

---

4 David L. Chapman, *Sandow the Magnificent: Eugen Sandow and the Beginnings of Body-building* (Urbana: University of Illinois Press, 2006), photograph between pp. 124 and 125.

5 Unidentified clipping, Scrapbook #83, Louis Armstrong Archive.

6 "[I] take care of my chops, teeth and everything," he said late in life. "I've gone through life trying to stay healthy." Jones and Chilton, *Louis*, 246.

7 Jones and Chilton, *Louis*, 246.

least a mile a day."[8] In winter he used the bathtub to hold his breath underwater, Houdini-style, for three minutes at a time, using a water-proof watch to time himself.[9] The wisdom of these preparatory measures, however, gave way to recklessness when he stepped into the spotlight. When it came to feeding the public's appetite for sensation, no asset was beyond sacrificing, not even the precious lips that made it all possible.

Despite the artistic and human costs of Armstrong's high-note exhibitions, the power and audacity of his approach to the upper register yielded a positive musical legacy. Through his relentless exertions he not only expanded the practical range of his instrument, but he also developed new expressive techniques that influenced future soloists and lead trumpet players in the 1930s and 1940s. Although Armstrong flirted with the high register during his time with Oliver and Henderson (and probably even before that, in New Orleans), the recorded beginnings of his serious high-note campaign can be dated to the spring of 1927. During this period he performed with his Hot Seven a swaggering solo on "S.O.L. Blues" (repeated almost note for note on "Gully Low Blues" the following day). This solo unveiled, in embryonic form, all the elements of Armstrong's mature high-note manner, an approach that ran stoutly against the grain of prevailing practice at the time, in both jazz and classical realms. It opened a new and exhilarating vision of what the trumpet could do, and how it could sound.

FIRST CHAIR AND THE UPPER REGISTER

Armstrong's interest in high notes was closely bound up with his aspiration to play first chair—and, no doubt, with his denial of that privilege by his early employers King Oliver and Fletcher Henderson. "If [Oliver] would have thought of it," Armstrong recalled in 1956, "he'd have let me play the lead. You notice all these records you hear more harmony...because his lead was weak....He should have put me to play the lead, knowing I had that first-chair tone."[10] Similarly, "Fletcher only let me play 3rd cornet," Armstrong complained, even though "he'd let me hit

8 Rex Stewart, *Jazz Masters of the Thirties* (New York: Macmillan, 1972), 41.

9 Ed Wallace, "Dixieland's Satchmo," *World Telegram and Sun Saturday Magazine*, 31 October 1953 [1958?], 6. "Louis Armstrong" vertical file, Institute of Jazz Studies.

10 Louis Armstrong, Voice of America interview, probably July 1956, part I, archive reel 93–001.9, Louis Armstrong Archive. Other Chicago musicians apparently thought Armstrong should play lead in the Creole Jazz Band as well. Baby Dodds recalled that Armstrong's New Orleans reputation was so strong that before he arrived in Chicago, "everybody wondered whether [Oliver would] let Louis play first or second. And Joe said, 'It's my band.

those high notes that the big prima-donnas, first-chair men, couldn't hit."[11] To be clear, Armstrong wasn't talking about high notes in a solo; rather, when high notes came along in an ensemble passage, he had to "jump up to first trumpet—hit them cats' high notes and get back to third."[12] But if Armstrong was already shouldering the most difficult aspect of first-chair playing—the high notes—why couldn't he do the rest of the job as well?

High notes represented an important consideration for a bandleader assigning seats in a cornet or trumpet section. Early in the twentieth century, the instrument's normal range was considerably narrower than it is now, and first-chair players—or lead players—were chosen in part for their facility in the upper register—a space from about G above the staff to high C at most.[13] The reason was strictly practical: arrangers usually assigned the highest notes of the chords to the first part in all sections so the melody could be clearly heard, rather than buried in the middle of the texture. Even though the first clarinet or saxophone might double the first cornet part, the cornet, being inherently louder, was obliged to play high notes with particular elegance and control. To be sure, other aspects of cornet technique were important to bandleaders as well, but the issue of range weighed heavily because of the seemingly universal difficulty of executing high notes on the instrument. A fluent and dependable upper register became an important emblem of superior cornet skill, and the honor of first chair was seen as its reward.

Armstrong got a close look at top New York lead players in the white bands that played opposite Henderson's each night at the Roseland Ballroom. Two impressed him especially: B. A. Rolfe, the first-chair player for Vincent Lopez, and Vic D'Ippolito, first trumpet for Sam Lanin. Twenty-five years later, Armstrong would name them both, along with King Oliver and another New Orleans player, "Old Man Morette," as the four trumpet players he most admired. An obscure player, Morette won

---

What am I going to do, play second?' So Louis joined the band in Chicago...and played second cornet under Joe." Baby Dodds as told to Larry Gara, *The Baby Dodds Story*, rev. ed. (Baton Rouge: Louisiana State University Press, 1992), 35. On the oral history recording *Satchmo and Me*, Lillian Hardin made a similar point, expressing frustration that Oliver only let Armstrong play the second part.

11   Jones and Chilton, *Louis*, 236.

12   Armstrong, Voice of America interview. Don Redman supported Armstrong's account. Frank Driggs, "Don Redman: Jazz Composer-Arranger," *The Jazz Review* 2 (November 1959): 9.

13   When referring to pitches played by trumpet players in the upper register, as here, I will do so according to B♭ trumpet key rather than concert key, because this is the standard practice among musicians. Thus, "high C" on the trumpet means high B♭ in concert.

Armstrong's admiration for the same reason as Rolfe and D'Ippolito: his ability "to hit those top notes every time." When Armstrong heard D'Ippolito at the Roseland, he "first commenced to notice how valuable a first chair man is. Vic had tone and he had punch; he was all but a hot man in that band."[14] This appreciation would stay with him throughout his life. In 1971 he remarked, "I always like to hear a good lead-trumpet in a big band—that first chair is so important."[15]

If D'Ippolito opened Armstrong's ears to the value of strong lead playing, it was Rolfe who kindled his desire to master the upper register. Born into a musical family led by a man who aspired (but failed) to do big things in show business, Benjamin Albert Rolfe (1876–1956) excelled at the cornet from a young age, and became a vaudeville headliner around the turn of the century. For his seemingly unnatural command of the extreme upper register, Rolfe was known as a stunt player. His act consisted of nine or ten brass musicians forming a semicircle while he stood in the center, playing solos. He typically decorated simple melodies with his specialty—high-register lip trills—while working his way up to the top of his range, usually double high C. In addition to playing in vaudeville and dance bands, Rolfe made it big in radio when he signed a ten-year contract in the 1930s with the Lucky Strike Corporation to play weekly broadcasts. At the peak of his success he was known to have earned $12,000 for a single night's performance, reason enough to inspire the emulation of admiring young players.[16] When at the Roseland Armstrong heard Rolfe take "Shadowland" an octave higher than it was written, he later recalled, "it inspired me to go after the high range."[17] It took a few years, though, for the inspiration to bear fruit. Armstrong admitted he waited until 1929 to make a recording in conscious imitation of Rolfe. On that record, "When You're Smiling," Armstrong plays at a medium-slow tempo the entire thirty-two-bar melody in the region of high C (climaxing on an F)—an astounding exhibition of endurance and control. "The way I look at it, that's the way a trumpet *should* play," he said.[18]

Armstrong plays high Cs and Ds in several of his recorded solos with Henderson, including "Naughty Man" (first take), "One of These Days," and "Tell Me, Dreamy Eyes" (second solo). It is hard to know what high

14 Peter Drew, "The Professional Viewpoint," *The Record Changer* (July–August 1950): 46–47.
15 Jones and Chilton, *Louis*, 242.
16 Glenn D. Bridges, *Pioneers in Brass* (Detroit: Sherwood Publications, 1965), appendix (no page numbers after p. 87).
17 M. Grupp, "How Armstrong Hits the High Ones," *Metronome* 54 (September 1938): 50.
18 Drew, "The Professional Viewpoint," 31.

notes he took over for the first-chair players in the section work. Although Henderson certainly knew of Armstrong's technical abilities, however, one can see why he kept him on third: Armstrong lacked the formal training and "legitimate" style normally required of a first-chair player in a society band. Teeming with idiosyncrasies, Armstrong's playing style was quirky, uneven, and absolutely unique. It was all right to individualize and jazz up a solo passage or an outchorus, but Henderson would have wanted stylistic precision and predictability on the more straightforward ensemble work. Armstrong the crowd-pleaser probably seemed a bit too rough-hewn a personality to entrust with the serious responsibilities of first chair. To Armstrong's protests at being undervalued, Henderson would only respond, "If you gonna be good someday, you'll take some lessons."[19]

Henderson's main first-chair player in the 1920s was Russell Smith, who joined the band shortly after Armstrong left in late 1925. Reedman Garvin Bushell considered Smith "one of the best legitimate trumpet players in the business," and bassist Wellman Braud said of him, "I never have heard a first-chair trumpet man like that in all my life. He *sings* first parts."[20] Although, as will be shown, Armstrong absorbed some legitimate trumpet skills and played first chair frequently in Chicago in the late 1920s, he never acquired the refinement characteristic of Smith's lead playing. This became evident in the spring of 1929 when Armstrong returned to New York. He was hired to play with Henderson's orchestra in the theater pit for Vincent Youmans's musical, *Horseshoes* (later called *Great Day*). According to the *New York Age*, the orchestra was to be "augmented by 20 musicians, strings, wood wind [*sic*] and French horns." Befitting Armstrong's by-then imposing reputation, the *Age* continued,

> Louis Armstrong was supposed to be first cornetist in the orchestra and Russell Smith, second cornetist. In fact, it is alleged they were so seated at a rehearsal, and after a number was played, either Dr. Felix, who is said to have arranged or composed the music, or the conductor, is alleged to have told Armstrong to change chairs with Smith. . . . The number was replayed and the decision was made that Armstrong was not adapted to the show business and his seat was declared vacant. Russell was retained as first trumpet.[21]

19 Armstrong, Voice of America interview.
20 Walter C. Allen, *Hendersonia: The Music of Fletcher Henderson and His Musicians*, Jazz Monographs, No. 4 (Highland Park, NJ: author, 1973), 166.
21 Allen, *Hendersonia*, 230.

Armstrong, in fact, may have left the show for his own reasons, as drummer Kaiser Marshall contends in the same article, but the account rings true in one sense: in contexts requiring classically oriented lead playing, like that of a Broadway show, Armstrong would have fallen well short of standards exemplified by such musicians as Smith.

Armstrong would have been acutely aware of the classical training expected of first-chair players and the corresponding high-class aura that surrounded them in musical settings. As a poorly educated young man from the South who even regarded himself as a "country boy," Armstrong interpreted Henderson's refusal to let him play lead in 1924–25 strictly as social prejudice: "Fletcher was so carried away with that society shit and his education he slipped by a small-timer and young musician— me—who wanted to do everything for him musically."[22] Henderson and his musicians expected Armstrong to play hot jazz because that fit with his New Orleans background. Playing first chair, on the other hand, not only seemed incompatible with Armstrong's basic playing style but must have run counter to Henderson's conception of him as socially uncouth, uneducated, and essentially unprepared for the responsibilities of society life, whether on the bandstand or off. But despite his fabulous success as a hot soloist, Armstrong resented being denied first chair, with all that that denial implied.

When Armstrong explained his frustrations to Lil over the phone, she told him to come home and play first cornet in her band, "which was an elevation for me," said Armstrong.[23] In joining Hardin's band, Armstrong may initially have thought simply to add lead-trumpet skills to his already impressive collection of solo techniques. Ultimately, however, he came to fuse the two performance strains, changing the way both lead and solo trumpet players approached their musical assignments.

THE SWITCH TO TRUMPET

Shortly after arriving back in Chicago, Armstrong switched from cornet to trumpet. Authorities generally agree that the change first appeared on record 28 May 1926, in three sides made with Erskine Tate, even though Armstrong had probably used the trumpet at the Vendome Theater for several months before that. One reason for the switch was purely musical. Since the trumpet has a cylindrical bore (as opposed to the cornet's

---

22 Quoted in Jones and Chilton, *Louis*, 237.
23 Jones and Chilton, *Louis*, 236.

conical bore) it produces an acoustically purer, more brilliant tone—one Armstrong heard as "mellow," "rich," and "pretty."[24] The cylindrical bore also gives the trumpet a more focused sound with less resistance, making it a congenial instrument for the taxing high-range excursions increasingly favored by Armstrong. As he himself put it, "the cornet works you harder."[25]

Another significant reason for the change had to do with the cultural meanings conveyed by the two instruments. Initially Armstrong switched because his section mate at the Vendome, Erskine Tate's brother, Jimmy, played the trumpet, and Erskine didn't like the way Armstrong's "stubby" little cornet looked alongside Jimmy's sleek trumpet.[26] In part, Armstrong took up the trumpet for the same reason he began wearing fine clothes: to elevate his social status and improve his image with the public. But the regal appearance of the trumpet was only one factor in this regard. In the 1920s the trumpet was widely regarded as a high-class instrument in musical terms, much more so than the cornet. Whereas cornets were used in concert bands, trumpets were used primarily in symphony orchestras, thereby benefiting from the rarefied ambiance of the concert hall. Possibly for that reason, "while [famous cornet soloists] were better known to the general public, the star trumpeters of the symphony became, as early as the second decade of the twentieth century, more celebrated within the musical world."[27] Armstrong sensed this hierarchy and was cowed by it. In New Orleans, he recalled, "only the big orchestras in the theaters had trumpet players in their brass sections." Accordingly, "we all thought you had to be a music conservatory man or some kind of a big muckity-muck to play the trumpet. For years I would not even try to play the instrument."[28] Perhaps, for Armstrong, finally picking up the trumpet did more than mitigate the physical problem of playing high notes. Perhaps adopting this powerful instrument was itself an act of audacity, helping to build the confidence bordering on arrogance that he would assuredly need to face down high F.[29]

24 Charles Edward Smith, "The Making of a King," *The Record Changer* 9, nos. 6 and 7 (1950): 21.
25 Smith, "The Making of a King," 21.
26 Meryman, "An Authentic American Genius," 112; Jones and Chilton, *Louis*, 237.
27 John Lawrence McCann, "A History of Trumpet and Cornet Pedagogy in the United States, 1840–1942" (PhD diss., Northwestern University, 1989), 24, quote on p. 31.
28 Louis Armstrong, *Satchmo: My Life in New Orleans* (New York: Prentice-Hall, 1954; reprint, New York: Da Capo, 1986), 213–14.
29 For more on this subject, see Kenney, *Chicago Jazz*, 42–43.

A year after taking up the trumpet, Armstrong began exploring the upper register with greater intensity. His explorations led him ultimately to found what might be called the modern school of lead trumpet playing in a jazz orchestra. Part of his influence came from simply playing higher than anyone had done before in jazz. A more important contribution, though, derived from the *way* he played in the upper register. Unlike those of his contemporaries, Armstrong's high notes were loud, fat, and full of power.

Classical players had already pioneered the extreme upper register. As early as the turn of the century, Herbert L. Clarke was playing up to high F on such virtuoso display pieces as "Carnival of Venice" and "Bride of the Waves." Recordings, however, show that his tone thinned out progressively as he went above high C. Armstrong's hero B. A. Rolfe manifested the same shrinking of tone as he ascended in range. On "Why Do I Love You," recorded with Vincent Lopez around 28 April 1925, Rolfe's high notes actually sound falsetto. This was not poor playing on the part of Clarke and Rolfe, but reflected normal practice among classically trained players in the early part of the century. A weak high register followed naturally from the pedagogy of the day regarding embouchure—the placement of the mouthpiece on the lips.

Following long-standing practice, early twentieth-century method books for cornet and trumpet admonished players to form a smile, drawing back the corners of the mouth before placing the mouthpiece, and to broaden the smile as the notes got higher. It was thought that stretching the lips created more rapid vibrations; as the vibrations sped up, the pitch would rise as well. The theory overlooked the byproduct of a thinner sound as the lips were stretched. A complementary theory, born around 1910, compounded the problem. In reaction against earlier teachings to press the instrument against the lips to ascend, a vast movement devoted to "nonpressure" took root. The aim was to protect the lips and allow them to vibrate freely. By the 1920s, nonpressure systems dominated studios and method books, particularly in Chicago.[30] As jazz-playing southern migrants moved north, many of them jumped on the bandwagon as well. After hiring Tommy Ladnier, Sam Wooding recalled being "very disappointed in his ability to blow: I found out from talking to him that it was because he was changing over from the pressure system of trumpet playing to the non-pressure system."[31] King Oliver sought relief from

---

30 McCann, "A History of Trumpet and Cornet Pedagogy," 70.

31 Art Napolean, "A Pioneer Looks Back: Sam Wooding 1967," *Storyville* 2, no. 9 (1967): 38.

TOP NOTES: "S.O.L. BLUES"/"GULLY LOW BLUES"   **97**

his pyorrhea in the nonpressure system as well, according to his wife, Stella.[32] Even Armstrong checked it out: "To find out what all that talk of the non-pressure system was about, he took some lessons from a German teacher down at Kimbal hall," in the Chicago College of Music.[33] (Whatever he heard, he disregarded it.)

Late in the decade, a backlash began against both of these theories. The campaign was led by symphony trumpeters, who demanded a higher "quality of tone, power, and consistency" than current practices would allow.[34] In 1928 William A. Thieck, former principal trumpet for the Minneapolis and San Francisco symphonies, assailed nonpressure methods:

> I would like to hear a trumpet section of a symphony orchestra play "Ein Helden Leben"...by Strauss using a non pressure device on their instruments, what a bunch of dead heroes there would be. I would like to hear a non pressure artist play Herbert Clarke's "Bride of the Waves."...Playing trumpet *without pressure* is the biggest nonsense, and I don't fear anyone in making this rather drastic statement.[35]

Thieck's point, generally accepted today, was that to play high with any strength, some pressure was required: "It is a simple matter to play high C without pressure if the lips are used correctly...*but the tonal quality or volume would be absolutely worthless in a ff phrase.*" At this date, however, Thieck was a voice crying in the wilderness. It would take another ten years before his views became widely accepted. Over that same period, the smile method was abandoned for the "pucker," an embouchure that helped keep the sound full in all registers. Equally important, teachers began to recognize the role of tongue movement in controlling pitch.

While pedagogues were developing new theories on how to attain a robust high register, Armstrong was leading the way in practice. Standing nearly alone in his ability to play powerful high notes, Armstrong astounded listeners with the sheer force of his playing. Rex Stewart, a cornet soloist for Duke Ellington, wrote of a cutting contest he witnessed between Armstrong and Cladys "Jabbo" Smith, the only trumpet player, according to many contemporaries, who posed a threat to Armstrong's supremacy. Smith played first. "And I'll say this," Stewart recalled,

32 Laurie Wright, "Stella Oliver Talks," *Storyville* 141 (March 1990): 107.
33 Ramsey and Smith, *Jazzmen*, 125.
34 McCann, "A History of Trumpet and Cornet Pedagogy," 118.
35 William A. Thieck, *Thieck's Daily Studies for Cornet and Trumpet* (Milwaukee, WI: Herman Bechler, 1928), 11, 12. Italics added.

"he was *blowing*." Smith could play high, too—up to "high F or G." But his high notes paled in comparison to Armstrong's. Bouncing "onto the opposite stage, immaculate in a white suit," Armstrong lifted his horn in response. "I've forgotten the tune," Stewart said, "but I'll never forget his first note."

> He blew a searing, soaring, altissimo, fantastic high note and held it long enough for every one of us musicians to grasp. Benny Carter, who has perfect pitch, said, "Damn! That's high F!"...Louis never let up that night, and it seemed that each climax topped its predecessor. Every time he'd take a break, the applause was thunderous.[36]

It wasn't the mere fact of having played a high F that impressed the audience (for Smith had done the same), but it was the mass and weight of Armstrong's note that made the difference. As cornetist Red Nichols put it, "Jabbo had a wide range, but his high notes were more falsetto, not full-blown like Louis'."[37]

Ray Nance, another Ellington trumpet player, recounted a similar experience from the 1920s about Armstrong's power in the upper register and its effect upon listeners. The occasion was Collegiate Night at the Savoy Ballroom in Chicago. Armstrong was playing "Tiger Rag" with Carroll Dickerson.

> He used to play those choruses and make one hundred high Cs. A cat in the wings was counting them. When Louis got to ninety-nine, he'd hit C and rattle it—eeeEE! By then, the people were hardly able to control themselves.... Then he'd rear back, roll his eyes, take a breath, and hit that note—bam! The whole place would be in pandemonium. I'm telling you, that was the greatest thrill I've ever had in my whole life.[38]

How did Armstrong play high notes with such strength? Being largely self-taught in trumpet technique, he mostly ignored prevailing ideas and unwittingly anticipated future orthodoxy. First, as photographs of his embouchure make clear, he did not pull back the corners of his mouth in a smile but puckered his lips. Approaching his instrument intuitively,

36 Stewart, *Jazz Masters of the Thirties*, 47.
37 Richard Hadlock, *Jazz Masters of the Twenties* (New York: Macmillan, 1972; reprint, New York: Da Capo, 1988), 43.
38 Jack Bradley, "Trumpet Fanfare," *Saturday Review*, 4 July 1970, 19. "Louis Armstrong" vertical file, William Ransom Hogan Jazz Archive, Tulane University.

he somehow stumbled onto an embouchure that was ahead of its time. Though he erred in pressing the mouthpiece too hard against the lips, according to trumpet virtuoso and pedagogue Wynton Marsalis, he at least used enough pressure to create the necessary seal behind his powerful high notes.[39] (At the Waif's Home, the reform school that taught him how to play at age twelve, Armstrong may have learned to press against the mouthpiece to go higher, as this had been standard pedagogy since the mid-nineteenth century.) Second, he played with maximum relaxation in the throat, allowing the air free passage in all registers. This was crucial, since the natural tendency is to constrict the muscles in the throat as one goes higher, paradoxically blocking the air stream and thwarting the ascent. In 1938 one M. Grupp, a specialist in "Wind Instrument Teaching," interviewed Armstrong to analyze his high-note technique. Grupp reported with some amazement:

> In studying his range, I had Louis play for me certain difficult tonguing and slurring intervals, from low F sharp to G above high C....I made a study of this natural player's instrumental and musical ability, of his personality, and physical make-up. With that hoarse-like voice of his, he impressed me as having one of the most relaxed speaking apparatuses I have ever known.... When "Hightoneking" [Grupp's nickname for Armstrong] plays the trumpet, he employs these physical equipments almost in the same relaxed manner as when speaking. This relaxation and cool-headedness...makes possible perfect co-ordination of his mind, breathing, lips, and tonguing apparatuses.[40]

Although Grupp may have been influenced by racial stereotypes in emphasizing the "naturalness" of Armstrong's technique, his point about the importance of relaxation when playing high notes was nevertheless insightful.

Third, Armstrong possessed a large (if stocky) physical frame, and trumpet players, like opera singers, have always derived breadth and power from imposing bodies. Indeed, his inclination to accent high notes may have been reinforced by his experience of listening to Enrico Caruso, the Italian tenor who revolutionized operatic singing style in the early years of the century.[41] Armstrong enjoyed listening to Caruso from

---

39 James Lincoln Collier–Wynton Marsalis debate, Jazz at Lincoln Center, 4 August 1994.

40 Grupp, "How Armstrong Hits the High Ones," 50, 55.

41 The connection between Armstrong and opera was first proposed by Joshua Berrett in his article, "Louis Armstrong and Opera," *Musical Quarterly* 76, no. 2 (1992): 216–41. I do not

the year he bought his first phonograph in 1918, and probably on other people's machines many years before that. He recalled that as a young street performer, "I used to sing tenor when I was twelve years old—with my hat around my ears—hit those big high notes like Caruso."[42] Caruso is said to have been the first to successfully bypass the break in the male vocal register, nullifying the qualitative distinction between "chest" and "head" voice. Whereas previous tenors sang falsetto in the region above the break, Caruso continued in the full strength of his voice as he ascended in register.[43] His ringing, majestic high notes captivated audiences and decisively altered vocal technique, laying the path for future powerhouse tenors like Placido Domingo and Luciano Pavarotti. One could make a similar statement about Armstrong and his influence on the trumpet.

"S.O.L. BLUES"/"GULLY LOW BLUES"

Armstrong's inclination to play high notes forcefully may have grown out of an expressive device he used a bit lower in register. Early on, he had developed a habit of approaching notes above the staff with a "rip"—a ragged, ascending glissando that led up to the note in question. Armstrong created the ascent in pitch by adjusting his air stream, oral cavity, and embouchure. The raggedness derived from harmonic partials—intermediate notes that sounded, briefly and vaguely, en route to the top note. Early Hot Five recordings display Armstrong's rips in abundance. His first break on "My Heart" begins with a rip to A (concert G) above the staff. Similarly, his solo on "Muskrat Ramble" features a rip to high B♭ in the second measure. And in the fourth phrase of his solo on "Big Butter and Egg Man" Armstrong rips to a G above the staff.

As these examples make clear, the rip had the effect of making the highest note a goal that Armstrong accented upon arrival. In this way his own performance practice set a precedent for emphasizing high notes rather than pulling back as the register increased. Still, in these early recordings he didn't hold the goal notes for very long. As the Hot

find most of his argument convincing, however. Particularly, his contention that operatic devices "were deeply internalized and fluently expressed in [Armstrong's] brilliant improvisations" is not supported, in my opinion, by the evidence he gives. I believe Berrett to be on firm ground in his general point that Armstrong's essentially vocal manner of playing melodies was bolstered by his appreciation of opera.

42 Louis Armstrong vertical file, Hogan Jazz Archive, Tulane University, New Orleans.

43 Salvatore Fucito and Barnet J. Beyer, *Caruso and the Art of Singing* (New York: Frederick A. Stokes, 1922), 144–51.

Five series progressed, Armstrong made three important changes in his approach: (1) he began ripping to higher notes, particularly high C; (2) he bolstered the accent on the goal note by lengthening its value and oftentimes adding a "shake" (an exaggerated vibrato effect that Armstrong evidently invented); and (3) he began smoothing out the rips by slightly depressing his valves, thereby eliminating intermediate partials and achieving a portamento effect like that of a trombone. In the absence of the former raggedness, Armstrong's rips became what writers call "half-valve glissandos."

These changes first began to coalesce in the Hot Seven recordings, from May 1927. As noted in chapter 2, Bud Freeman speculated that the experience of playing with Brown and McGraw and other dancers at the Sunset Café stimulated Armstrong to probe the upper register: "Louie began to develop a high range nobody had ever heard in Chicago."[44] Perhaps the kinetic excitement of the dancers' steps inspired Armstrong to strive for something similar on the trumpet, sending him upward with greater intensity than before. Whatever the reason, a change did occur. Compared with the session that produced "Big Butter and Egg Man" six months earlier, the Hot Sevens reveal an Armstrong newly energized in the upper register. His preoccupation with high notes is everywhere evident, beginning with the sustained high C (with a shake) on "Willie the Weeper" and his sustained high B (with a shake) on "Alligator Crawl." His highest note from this period marks a moment of real drama: his rip to high D at the climactic end of his stop-time solo on "Potato Head Blues." One can hear his budding interest in playing melodies an octave higher than written, on "Alligator Crawl," in which he makes a coy, abortive attempt (were he to continue he would have been forced up to high F♯), and on "Weary Blues," where he quotes "Twelfth Street Rag" briefly in the region around high C. On "Willie the Weeper," "Potato Head Blues," and "Keyhole Blues," he also inaugurates a new practice of playing outchoruses an octave higher than usual, often as a dynamic continuation of a solo chorus that ends in the upper register.

But the most impressive high-note display, certainly, is on "S.O.L. Blues" and its twin "Gully Low Blues," which I will consider as a single performance. In preparation, let us briefly consider the meaning of high C in the 1920s. Though no big deal today, high C then represented the peak of a trumpet's written range and the fondest dream of every young player. "An accomplished Trumpet player can play...as high as D♭[concert]," admitted Arthur Lange in his book *Arranging for the Modern Dance*

44 Freeman, "The Father and His Flock," 16.

Orchestra (1926), but this range "is not practical to write."[45] Lange's suggested range went to G above the staff, with A and B♭ (high C) in parentheses. With a touch of derision, symphony trumpeter William Thieck noted that "most Cornet or Trumpet players' aim is to get high C. No tone on the Trumpet or Cornet is mentioned so often among beginners, also semi professionals, as high C." Yet even Thieck saw it as a kind of barrier: "Occasionally one finds a player who will do stunts with...extremely high tones but they belong to the class of the phenomenal and should be no guide to the average student."[46] Not surprisingly, Armstrong's high Cs stirred excitement, even as late as 1930. In that year a New York reporter marveled that Armstrong "blows a mean trumpet, and we don't mean maybe, hitting high C with apparent ease and comfort."[47] A few weeks later, a Chicago reporter wrote that "Louis Armstrong, 'World's Greatest Cornetist' is knockin' 'em cold at the Regal and will continue to trumpet 'high C' to thousands of riotous fans now storming the South Side Palace of Pleasure to hear him."[48]

This was the period when Armstrong was unleashing high Cs by the hundred. In his haughty, unequivocal command of that register on "S.O.L. Blues," however, he performed a stunt in some ways no less impressive. The solo is dominated by five consecutive high Cs, each sustained for several beats at a slow tempo, each of strapping tone and volume and energized by Armstrong's trademark shake (example 4.1). Each high C is immediately followed by up to two octaves of plunging arpeggios, which—in contrast to the constancy of the high notes—change in shape and harmonic content from one to the next. The very idea of a series of lofty plateaus followed by precipitous descents is a powerful one. Other trumpet players in the 1920s were incapable of executing the high-note part of the solo, and the effect would have been lost if another instrument—such as clarinet or piano—played it. The effectiveness of Armstrong's solo stemmed directly from those blazing, shuddering high Cs, symbols of technical conquest.

Armstrong begins each high C with a brief but vigorous upward rip, smoothed out somewhat through half-valving, which endows the solo with the insistent urgency of a siren. Half-valving allowed Armstrong, in theory, to extend the upward lead-in indefinitely, producing a suspense that called for even greater emphasis upon the arrival of the goal note. Moreover, when the valves on a trumpet are depressed halfway the

45 Lange, *Arranging for the Modern Dance Orchestra*, 46.
46 Thieck, *Thieck's Daily Studies*, 10, 2.
47 *Zit's Theatrical Newspaper*, 29 January 1930, in Scrapbook #83, Louis Armstrong Archive.
48 *Chicago Savoyager*, 8–17 February 1930, in Scrapbook #83, Louis Armstrong Archive.

EXAMPLE 4.1   Louis Armstrong and His Hot Seven, "S.O.L. Blues," 13 May 1927, Louis Armstrong's solo.

tone sounds muffled, for unlike the trombone, the trumpet produces glissandos artificially.[49] Armstrong's half-valve ascents, therefore, were accompanied by an escalating need for sonorous release—for the unhindered open sound of a trumpet resonating in one of the seven standard valve combinations. That release occurred when Armstrong reached his intended high note, which he invariably executed in an ecstatic fortissimo, shattering the built-up tension. An outstanding example of this practice appears during the middle of Armstrong's chorus on "I Gotta Right to Sing the Blues," recorded on 26 January 1933. Following a string of repeated high Cs, Armstrong begins the two-bar break with a descending glissando, then reverses direction and for a measure and a half inches gradually upward to land on an exultant high E on the downbeat of the next section.

Although such dramatic half-valve glissandos do not appear in the Hot Five series, the same principles are at work in incipient form. After the piano solo on "Don't Jive Me," recorded 28 June 1928, Armstrong leads the ensemble on sustained high Cs, blowing the first one so hard that he goes sharp. Armstrong precedes each high C with a tiny half-valve scoop. Too brief to be called glissandos, the scoops nevertheless dramatize the high notes. Because half-valving mutes the tone, and since releasing the valve is a continuous (rather than a discrete) process,

49 See Gunther Schuller, *The Swing Era: The Development of Jazz, 1930–1945* (New York: Oxford University Press, 1989), 183.

Armstrong's goal note emerges as "wah"—as though he were using a plunger. Thus, he actually employs half-valve effects in place of articulation with the tongue. Instead of hitting high C squarely with a "dah" or "tah," he witholds the tongue attack and lets the release of the valve on "wah" do the work for him. The rapidly expanding vowel in the *w* sound, combined with the scoop's rise in pitch, accentuate the goal note more powerfully than could the abrupt consonants *d* or *t*. Preceded by half-valve scoops, Armstrong's high Cs come at the listener like massive objects hurtling from a distance. The half-valving on "Don't Jive Me," it should be noted, is much smoother than on "S.O.L. Blues." Indeed, one can see, by comparing these two pieces, how he eventually found his way to "I Gotta Right to Sing the Blues."

The lyrics to "S.O.L. Blues" and "Gully Low Blues" may shed light on the meaning of Armstrong's solo.[50] On the latter recording, he sings of romantic frustrations that may have hit his wife, Lil Hardin, playing piano at the session, painfully close to home:

Now, momma, momma, momma, why do you treat me so?
[repeated]
   (I know why you treat me so bad!)
You treat me mean, baby, just because I'm "gully low."

Now, momma—If you listen, baby, I'll tell you something you don't know.
[repeated]
If you just give me a break and take me back, I won't be "gully" no mo.'

The term "gully low" referred to an extreme form of "lowdown," which could mean uncouth and unsophisticated as well as immoral or dirty.[51] "Lowdown" was used in a positive sense to characterize deeply honest and expressive jazz and blues. But Hardin and her socially aspiring family would not have approved of its manifestation in social settings.[52] As is

50 For a different, though related, perspective on "Gully Low Blues," see Charles Hiroshi Garrett, *Struggling to Define a Nation: American Music and the Twentieth Century* (Berkeley: University of California Press, 2008), 83–120.
51 Ramsey and Smith, *Jazzmen*, 12.
52 Hardin's mother, Dempsy, disapproved of all aspects of lowdown culture, including music. Dempsy considered the blues to be "wuthless immoral music, played by wuthless, immoral loafers expressin' their vulgar minds with vulgar music." James Lincoln Collier, *Louis Armstrong: An American Genius* (New York: Oxford University Press, 1983), 111.

shown in chapter 6, she was constantly upbraiding Armstrong for small breaches of etiquette, including the deep-seated habits he had acquired in the rough part of New Orleans where he grew up. Over several years the contention pushed them apart, eventually ending their marriage in the 1930s. During their on-again, off-again relationship in the mid-1920s, though, Armstrong may have promised "I won't be 'gully' no mo'" many times in an effort to pacify Lil.[53]

So far, so good. After singing this lyric, however, Armstrong lifts his horn and plays that cocky, ebullient solo, full of lowdown idiosyncrasies: shakes, half-valve rips, bulging high Cs, to say nothing of the soaking wet bluesiness of the falling arpeggios—probably just the sorts of thing that in 1929 would get him fired from his job playing first chair in *Great Day*. The solo, in other words, repudiates the very idea of social reform, making a mockery of the singer's promises. But through the power of those high Cs it does so with a towering, masculine authority that both exalts lowdown values and negates the tremulous abasement of that last line: "I won't be gully no mo'."[54] The cruel irony of the solo is reinforced by the contrasting lyrics on "S.O.L. Blues" (which communicate a G-rated version of the message coded in the abbreviated title: "Shit-Out-of-Luck Blues"):

Now I'm with you sweet mama as long as you have the bucks,
    (Bucks, bucks, bucks, bucks—I mean money, mama!)
[repeated]
When the bucks run out, sweet mama, I mean you out of luck.
    (Out of luck, mama!)

Thomas Brothers writes of the fierce pride and independence, bordering on defiance, that Armstrong learned from the church women who raised him in New Orleans.[55] Although Brothers speaks of these values in the context of race, they applied to gender as well. From the pimps and gamblers, Armstrong learned this bloodless lesson about relationships: "Never worry over no one woman—no matter how pretty or sweet she

---

53 Baby Dodds remembered that Armstrong had written a tune called "Gully Low" while he was playing with King Oliver. Dodds and Gara, *The Baby Dodds Story*, 36. If this is the same piece, it may have been inspired by Armstrong and Hardin's early relationship together, during which the conflict over Armstrong's lack of sophistication may have been even more acute.

54 For more on the trumpet and high notes as symbols of masculinity, see Gabbard, "Signifyin(g) the Phallus," 138–59.

55 Brothers, *Louis Armstrong's New Orleans*, 46–51.

may be. Any time she gets down wrong, and ain't playing the part of a wife—get yourself somebody else, also.—And get another woman much better than the last one at all times."[56] Armstrong's occasionally misogynistic comments about his wives or women generally are in line with this philosophy, which fits this second set of lyrics much better than the first one.[57] Thus, the two lyrics are Janus-faced twins, one telling the truth and the other a falsehood. The trumpet solo tells the truth in both.

MAJESTIC STYLE

Let's consider, in closing, some of the paths to which this extraordinary solo led. First, through such performances Armstrong changed the practical range of his instrument. Like Roger Bannister shattering running standards with the four-minute mile, Armstrong demystified high C for younger players, who began to see it as a starting point to greater heights rather than as a goal in itself. In school "we played all Louis Armstrong's things note for note," recalled Cat Anderson, Duke Ellington's high-note specialist from the 1930s onward. "All the trumpet players played 'Shine' and made a hundred Cs with the F on top."[58]

Second, Armstrong inspired a multitude of swing trumpet soloists to adopt the expressive devices he used in the upper register, devices that together constituted what my old teacher Mark Tucker called *majestic style*. This brawny, aggressive style of playing, typified by full-bodied high notes, soaring half-valve glissandos, and electrifying shakes, perfectly suited the romantic showmanship of the swing era. Armstrong performances in this idiom, such as "I Gotta Right to Sing the Blues," can be seen as the direct ancestors of such later bravura performances as Bunny Berigan's "I Can't Get Started" (1936), Ziggy Elman's "And the Angels Sing" (1939), Cootie Williams's "Concerto for Cootie" (third "open horn" theme) (1940), and Ray Nance's "Take the 'A' Train" (second "open horn" solo) (1941). Williams, of course, became famous for continuing the plunger-mute tradition begun in the Duke Ellington band by Bubber

---

56 Armstrong, *Louis Armstrong in His Own Words*, 96.
57 Bruce Raeburn, "Louis and Women," Louis Armstrong Symposium, University of North Carolina–Chapel Hill, 2 March 2001. Reprinted on the Web site http://bestofneworleans. com/gyrobase/Content?oid=oid%3A32924; accessed 17 February 2010.
58 Stanley Dance, "Louis Armstrong, American Original," *Saturday Review*, 4 July 1970, 13; clipping in Armstrong verticle file, Hogan Jazz Archive.

Miley. But "with my open horn playing," he admitted, "my influence was Louis Armstrong."[59]

Third, first-chair jazz trumpet players in the 1930s and 1940s began assimilating characteristics of majestic style into their lead playing with the ensemble, either through arrangers' notated instructions or through their own initiative.[60] It took a while for Armstrong's lead-playing followers to match his strength in the high range. As late as 1938 white trumpet star Harry James remarked, "I've never heard a trumpet player whose tone didn't thin out considerably when he played above high C—with the exception of Louis's."[61] By the 1940s, though, lead players had begun superceding him. In *The Swing Era* Schuller reminisces nostalgically about listening night after night to Charlie Barnet's band, one of the few swing bands still operating after the war, but, along with Dizzy Gillespie's and Stan Kenton's, "clearly one of the most exciting" of the period. Schuller especially marveled at Barnet's first trumpeter Al Killian, who routinely unleashed "full, round, fat altissimo B♭s and As."[62] The description recalls Rex Stewart's characterization of Armstrong's duel with Jabbo Smith. Postwar lead players continued to build on Armstrong's early 1930s style. Snooky Young, widely regarded as a founder of modern lead style, acknowledged Armstrong as his "main influence."[63] Even Maynard Ferguson, not technically a first-chair player but probably the century's preeminent high-note specialist, and one who thoroughly exploited majestic style devices, said that his main influences were "Louis Armstrong and my mother."[64]

After being denied first chair by Oliver, Henderson, and the conductor of *Great Day*, it must have been sweet revenge for Armstrong to observe his own special approach to "top notes" adopted as the standard by virtually every lead player in the country. That this approach can be traced back to recordings like "S.O.L. Blues" reveals a prophetic innovation of the Hot Five and Hot Seven recordings that is not generally attributed to them.

---

59 Cootie Williams, "Reminiscing with Cootie," interview by Eric Townley, *Storyville* 71 (June–July 1977): 172.

60 George L. Hitt, "The Lead Trumpet in Jazz (1924–1970)" (PhD diss., Indiana University, 1976), 49, 67.

61 Harry James, "Jammin' with James," *Metronome* 54 (August 1938): 13.

62 Schuller, *The Swing Era*, 722.

63 Dance, "Louis Armstrong," 13.

64 www.maynardferguson.com; accessed 5 September 2009.

CHAPTER 5

SWEET MUSIC
"SAVOY BLUES"

(13 DECEMBER 1927)

> You got to like playing pretty things if you're ever going to be any
> good blowing your horn.
>
> — LOUIS ARMSTRONG

IN 1955, A BANQUET WAS HELD at Harlem's Savoy Ballroom honoring the thirty or so NAACP lawyers who had worked on *Brown v. Board of Education*, the landmark Supreme Court decision, handed down the previous year, to outlaw segregation in the public schools. One of the lawyers, Charles L. Black Jr., was a Columbia law professor with an unlikely background for such a case. Black was a white Texan who, by his own account, was all too well acquainted with the "good old boy" racism of the South. One night in 1931, however, he heard Louis Armstrong perform live, and was transformed. The experience hooked him on black jazz, effected a sea change in his views on race, and put him on the road that led to *Brown*. He was meditating on this history the night he arrived home from the banquet with his wife, Barbara. "We were quiet on the elevator, quiet into the vestibule, the living room. I went over to the record-player, and put on Louis's *Savoy Blues*, the 1927 OKeh....I listened to it all through; Barbara stood silent behind me. When it was over, I stayed still a moment more, then I turned to her and said, 'Well, baby, thank God, that's one thing I didn't go back on.' " His choice of commemorative music was not accidental. "I came home from that party and played the *Savoy Blues*," he repeated. "Not another record. Just that one." Why? "Perhaps it was... only an imagination of mine. But in the trumpet on that record, just that one, I thought I heard something said... gently, without stridency or self-pity: 'We are being wronged, grievously, heavily, bewilderingly wronged. We don't know why or what to do. Is anyone listening? Is there anyone to come in and help us?'... That is what I heard in his horn—so triumphant in other places and so full of glory—in the *Savoy Blues* of 1927."[1]

Black's very personal response to "Savoy Blues" bespeaks an intimacy, a pathos, and a subtlety of expression in Armstrong's performance that one does not always associate with 1920s jazz. Others have responded in similarly complex ways. According to James Lincoln Collier, "Armstrong's playing on 'Savoy Blues' expresses a mood of quiet tenderness, shading into outright sadness, that was to become increasingly evident in his work."[2] Likewise, Edward Brooks considers the piece "tender and introspective," displaying "a wide range of moods," and Lawrence Gushee praises Armstrong's "deeply affecting solo."[3] However one describes it, Armstrong's playing on "Savoy Blues" marks a clear departure from his previous work. The new features can be related most profitably to an idiom known as sweet jazz, the respectable cousin of hot jazz, Armstrong's notorious mother tongue. Not that Armstrong abandoned the latter for the former. Like other upwardly mobile black musicians of his time, he simply began absorbing sweet elements into his fundamentally hot manner. He may have done so to boost his own musical and social standing. But if so, it is striking that he chose to make the change not in popular songs, the usual vehicles for sweet expression, but in the blues, the roughest and most disreputable genre of the day.

THE ALLURE OF THE SWEET

Whether the names were chosen by E. A. Fearn, Ralph Peer, or the bandleader himself, Armstrong's recording groups were called the Hot Five and Hot Seven for good reason. Presenting a music of hard-swinging

1 Charles L. Black Jr., "My World with Louis Armstrong," *Yale Law Journal* 95 (1986): 1595–1600.
2 Collier, *Louis Armstrong*, 186–87.
3 Brooks, *Young Louis Armstrong*, 419, 420; Gushee, "The Improvisation of Louis Armstrong," 308.

rhythmic excitement, bluesy expressiveness, raucous polyphony, and at least the appearance of improvised spontaneity, these bands seemed to epitomize "hot," even in the 1920s. Traditionally, writers have emphasized the aesthetic reasons for Armstrong's choice of band and repertory. After playing arranged dance music for a year with Fletcher Henderson, Bill Russell wrote, "Louis just had to 'stretch out,' and that meant with a five-piece, New Orleans barrel-house bunch."[4] But Armstrong (or his handlers) probably based their decision on economic considerations as much as anything else. His likely customers, working-class blacks, preferred music connected with their own racial heritage: southern jazz and the blues. This preference had become apparent as early as 1923, when in that year alone King Oliver made over forty-five records for four companies while Erskine Tate's Vendome Theater Orchestra recorded only five sides in the entire decade after a much-publicized debut. New Orleans-style jazz continued to be popular two years later, and Armstrong wisely chose to capitalize on that popularity.

Nevertheless, for a moment—however brief—things might have gone in a different direction. John Chilton says that E. A. Fearn, the OKeh manager, initially wanted Armstrong to record music in the manner of Paul Whiteman.[5] Even though this idea was rejected, the story suggests a respect and admiration for Whiteman that was undoubtedly real. Routine assaults on jazz in the press posed a serious threat to musicians' livelihoods. Even the *Chicago Defender* published a cartoon on the front page placing "expensive night life (cabarets)" high up on a list of vices leading "misguided youth" on a "death march"— worse than moonshine, street corner gangs, petty larceny, pool rooms, and gambling, but not as bad as banditry or murder.[6] In response to such attacks, Whiteman and other like-minded bandleaders developed sweet jazz, a type of music that retained a spirit of novelty and mild boisterousness while at the same time weakening the music's perceived connection with immorality, crime, musical illiteracy, and black culture. Also known as "dicty" or "society" music, sweet jazz submitted to a sort of European-style discipline. Reformers like Whiteman believed that "orchestrating" jazz, for starters, would elevate the sense of refinement and decorum. Sweet bands played a music of lilting melodies,

4   Ramsey and Smith, *Jazzmen*, 130.
5   John Chilton, liner notes, *Louis Armstrong: The Hot Fives, vol. 1*, Columbia Jazz Masterpieces, CBS Records, 1988, 44049.
6   *Defender*, 10 December 1927, 1.

rich harmonies and orchestration, and serene rhythms, together with occasional novelty devices.

The idea of an ambitious young black musician embracing sweet jazz would not have been shocking in the 1920s. Sweet jazz, after all, connoted sophistication, and at the height of the Harlem Renaissance, a movement to elevate black artistic achievements, such considerations mattered. In an essay titled "Jazz at Home" in Alain Locke's landmark volume *The New Negro* (1925), J. A. Rogers presented the black elite view of jazz. Rogers envisioned a "great future" for the music, not through the work of roughnecks like King Oliver and Willie "The Lion" Smith, but through high-class orchestras "like those of Will Marion Cook, Paul Whiteman, Sissle and Blake, Sam Stewart, Fletcher Henderson, [and] Vincent Lopez." Although this roster included black bands, Rogers had to admit that "because of the difficulties of financial backing, these expert combinations have had to yield ground to white orchestras of the type of Paul Whiteman and Vincent Lopez, organizations that are now demonstrating the finer possibilities of jazz music."[7]

Black musicians from middle- and working-class backgrounds, to be sure, took a rather more ambivalent view of sweet jazz. In his column "The Musical Bunch," Dave Peyton touts the virtues of "high class" music and "polite syncopation," and just as often lambastes the "loud, discordant, barbaric" kind of jazz, whatever that may be. Yet he expounds contradictory opinions on both, rendering his true views all but opaque. In one issue he praises "the great Whiteman" for redeeming jazz with "his new syncopation."[8] But upon receiving a copy of Whiteman's book on jazz, he asks archly: "What does Whiteman know about jazz?"[9] Sometimes he denounces improvisation, admonishing black musicians to "play the score and stop faking."[10] Other times he defends black improvisers against white note readers: "The white musician does everything mechanically; he adheres to theory, while our musicians who know how to improvise add to the composer's idea."[11] Frequently, Peyton predicts that "polite syncopation" in the Whiteman

---

7 J. A. Rogers, "Jazz at Home," in *The New Negro: An Interpretation*, ed. Alain Locke (New York: Albert & Charles Boni, 1925; reprint, New York: Arne Press and the *New York Times*, 1968), 221.

8 *Defender*, 29 October 1927, 9.

9 *Defender*, 22 May 1926, 6.

10 *Defender*, 29 October 1927, 9.

11 *Defender*, 18 September 1926, 6.

mold "will thrive and be enjoyed by the great majority of music lovers in America."[12] But occasionally he throws up his hands and acknowledges the hard truth: "The crowds seem to go where the 'noise' is and I guess, after all, it is what the crowd says that counts.... Let the box office ring."[13] These positions may somehow be reconcilable, but the very need to reconcile them shows the complexity of Peyton's thoughts and feelings.

As will be shown in chapter 6, Armstrong experienced similar—if much stronger—ambivalence about embracing high-class values in his music and his life. What he could not do, however, was to ignore the sweet sounds proliferating around him. In the fall of 1927 their accumulating presence in his mind finally spilled over into his music in a pronounced manner. This sudden transfusion may have taken place through the intermediary of Guy Lombardo, an ultrasweet bandleader whose music Armstrong began hearing regularly for the first time.

GUY LOMBARDO'S MOOD MUSIC

Italian Canadian bandleader Guy Lombardo and His Royal Canadians came to Chicago in the fall of 1927 after building a regional reputation in Cleveland. Performing nightly at the Granada Café in downtown Chicago, the band at first generated little interest. In November Lombardo prevailed upon Al Quodbach, the owner, to broadcast their performances on the radio. Station WBBM agreed to fifteen minutes of airtime a night. But after the band signed off on the first night, callers jammed the phone lines asking for more. The station announcer immediately called Lombardo and asked him to play until the station went off the air at 1:00 A.M. People who heard the brief broadcast began coming into the Granada that same night. Events of the next day confirmed that, by word of mouth, Lombardo had literally become an "overnight sensation."[14] Offers of sponsorship came in from Wrigley's Chewing Gum and Florsheim Shoes. Callers deluged station WBBM, and on the second night the Granada was packed. Thus began Lombardo's meteoric rise to the status of pop music phenomenon.

12 *Defender*, 7 August 1926, 6.
13 *Defender*, 3 April 1926, 6.
14 Booton Herndon, *The Sweetest Music This Side of Heaven: The Guy Lombardo Story* (New York: McGraw-Hill, 1964), 63–68.

Over the next few years, Lombardo became famous for a particularly sweet and highly individual sound emphasizing slow tempos, fast
vibrato (especially in the saxophones), and staccato phrasing. Rich in
unabashed sentimentality, his music seemed ideally fitted for love songs.
Modifying a phrase coined by an enthusiastic reviewer, Lombardo in
1929 began advertising "the sweetest music this side of heaven." The ad
copy continued:

> It has been said of the dance music of GUY LOMBARDO that it
> smoulders and glows like a living coal . . . now soft with a lilting cadence
> of a dreamy melody . . . now vivid with pulsating jazz rhythms. In turn
> seductive and tumultuous, alternately tender and unrestrained, it is
> proving the season's outstanding musical sensation.[15]

Although claiming obligatory competence as a jazz artist, Lombardo
revealed his true nature with words like soft, lilting, dreamy, seductive,
and tender. Once, on a vaudeville bill early in his career, he tried to do
a comedy show and flopped. The angry manager "told Lombardo that
he had been hired to provoke sighs, not belly laughs.... By and large,
Lombardo has concentrated on provoking sighs—romantic or nostalgic—ever since."[16] To enhance the mood of his dreamy-eyed dancers,
Lombardo would dim the lights to almost total obscurity. The songwrit-
ing team of Schwartz and Dietz wrote "Dancing in the Dark" after spend-
ing an evening with Lombardo.[17]

As early as 1928, Dave Peyton wrote that Lombardo had "a great following among our people," meaning Chicago's black community.[18] This
following included jazz musicians. According to Lebert Lombardo, the
band's trumpet player, Quodbach would not allow black patrons at the
Granada. So "all the colored musicians, like Louis [Armstrong] and Cab
Calloway," would come to the parking lot and listen through the high
open windows. "They loved the sound of the saxophones." Lombardo's
men returned the compliment by coming by the Savoy Ballroom to meet
Armstrong and hear him play.[19] Finally, they must have obtained per-
mission from Quodbach to bring Armstrong into the Granada, because

15 Saul Richman, *Guy* (New York: RichGuy Publishing, 1978), 77.
16 E. J. Kahn, "Powder Your Face with Sunshine, Part 2," *The New Yorker*, 12 January 1957, 40.
17 E. J. Kahn, "Powder Your Face with Sunshine, Part 1," *The New Yorker*, 5 January 1957, 48.
18 *Defender*, 29 December 1928, 6.
19 Beverly Fink Cline, *The Lombardo Story* (Don Mills, Ontario: Musson, 1979), 43.

one week in October 1928 that is exactly what happened, according to Peyton's delighted report:

> Louis says he was never lauded and treated any better anywhere in his life as he was by this famous orchestral group.... The minute the cornet king entered was the signal for a chord from the orchestra, Guy Lombardo made famous over the air. The boys were given a table in juxtaposition to the bandstand. They were dined and wined until the wee hours of the morning.[20]

By Armstrong's account, he actually sat in with the band that night, both playing and singing.[21]

Armstrong later claimed—repeatedly and with great emphasis—that Guy Lombardo's band was his all-time favorite. Critics were appalled. How could Armstrong, one of the greatest jazz musicians, prefer the much-maligned "King of Corn," a bandleader whose music was, as one critic famously put it, the "antithesis of jazz"? Searching for answers to this baffling question, some dismissed the apparent lapse in taste as a curious eccentricity, like Armstrong's evangelizing for the laxative Swiss Kriss or his fondness for pens with green ink. Others saw it as a shrewd sell-out, an unprincipled attempt to expand his audience beyond true believers in the jazz community. In a recent study, Elijah Wald argues that Armstrong's love of Lombardo reflected a broader appreciation of white traditions generally, including European classical music and brass bands.[22] Armstrong himself gave the simplest explanation: "[Lombardo's] band plays the tune, they put that melody there and it's beautiful. You can't find another band that can play a straight lead and make it sound that good."[23]

A close look at the origins of Armstrong's admiration suggests that the explanation may be even more mundane than that. Armstrong discovered Lombardo early on, when the latter began broadcasting from the Granada Café. Every Sunday night Armstrong and his bandmates would race home from their gig at the Savoy Ballroom—home, that is, to "the Ranch," a flat they had rented for their "private sessions," Armstrong's

20 *Defender*, 13 October 1928, 6.
21 Herndon, *The Sweetest Music This Side of Heaven*, 73.
22 Elijah Wald, "Louis Armstrong Loves Guy Lombardo! Acknowledging the Smoother Roots of Jazz," *Jazz Research Journal* 1 (2007): 129–45.
23 Collier, *Louis Armstrong*, 220.

euphemism for romantic liaisons.[24] ("All the colored musicians" used to go to the Ranch, recalled white trumpeter Wild Bill Davison, who went himself with Armstrong on occasion.[25]) Once inside, where the icebox was filled with steaks, beer, and other refreshments, the first thing they did was turn on the radio to catch the last hour of Lombardo's live broadcast. "There we would listen to the sweetest music this side of heaven," Armstrong recalled. "With the lights down real low—and no one would say a word while they would play...Guy Lombardo had us spellbound."[26] It is possible, I suppose, that Armstrong and his male friends listened to Lombardo "with the lights down real low," but this loaded phrase seems far more apt to suggest they had wives or girlfriends with them, and that the Ranch and the music were both being used for their intended purpose: to pitch woo.

Armstrong's warm description of the social context in which he gained his appreciation for Lombardo's music helps to explain the depth and durability of his admiration. If Armstrong seemed uncomprehending when interviewers questioned his devotion to Lombardo, it may be because he didn't see the issue through the same doctrinaire lens. The dichotomies of hot versus sweet and hip versus square that exercised critics might have had little relevance for a music used primarily as a cue for lovemaking. Every generation has its syrupy make-out music, whether Jackie Gleason in the 1950s or Bread in the 1970s. If Lombardo served this purpose for the young Armstrong, the associated emotions and memories must have been powerful. This primal connection would also explain how sweet elements began coloring Armstrong's own music so effortlessly, without a trace of artifice or incongruity, around the same time. The change may appear sudden in hindsight, but in fact these elements complemented and reinforced developments in Armstrong's playing that had been under way for years.

EXPANDING BLUES HARMONY

Long before Lombardo came to the Granada Café, Armstrong began experimenting with harmonic resources that would prepare him for his sweet breakthrough on "Savoy Blues." Somewhat surprisingly, this

---

24 Herndon, *The Sweetest Music This Side of Heaven*, 72.
25 Eddie Condon and Richard Gehman, eds., *Eddie Condon's Treasury of Jazz* (New York: Dial Press, 1956), 157.
26 Herndon, *The Sweetest Music This Side of Heaven*, 73–74.

path led not so much through earlier Hot Five recordings as through Armstrong's many accompaniments to blues singers. Between 1924 and 1927, he recorded with such major figures as Bessie Smith, Clara Smith, Trixie Smith, and Alberta Hunter, as well as with lesser-known singers like Maggie Jones, Blanche Calloway, and Hociel Thomas. For most of his accompaniments Armstrong adopted a traditional melodic strategy inherited from King Oliver and other New Orleans predecessors. This strategy was centered around blue notes, stock phrases, and a dialect consisting of bends, dips, smears, and other mutations of pitch that made blue notes the logical result of a malleable idiom rather than arbitrary deformations of the major scale. Armstrong's emphasis on blue notes, his use of what today is called the *blues scale*, conformed to a style of playing known in the 1920s as "gutbucket." His guitarist on the early Hot Fives, Johnny St. Cyr, explained the meaning of the term: "In the fish markets in New Orleans the fish cleaners keep a large bucket under the table where they clean the fish, and as they do this they rake the guts in this bucket." Describing a piece as "gutbucket," he continued, "makes it a lowdown blues."[27]

One advantage of emphasizing the blues scale lies in its wide applicability. At any point in a twelve-bar blues progression, the blues scale in the tonic key (e.g., C–E♭–F–F♯–G–B♭ in the key of C) will fit, chameleon-like, into the background harmony. This versatile harmonic quality of blues-scale playing greatly simplifies the task of improvisation. Many successful blues solos reiterate fragments of the blues scale for whole choruses at a time. For horn-playing blues accompanists the task becomes simpler still. Usually the accompanist provides fills between the singer's phrases in call-and-response fashion. Playing every two bars in this manner, blues accompanists find themselves perpetually on the tonic chord (in the simplest blues progressions), while the singer occupies the measures that change harmonically. The limited nature of blues harmony for accompanists allowed players like Oliver and Tommy Ladnier to focus exclusively on other musical elements, such as timbre (through muted effects) and pitch (through repeated riffs and lip bends).

Given Armstrong's prodigal inventiveness, it is not surprising that the blues scale, by itself, proved insufficiently stimulating as a melodic source. Mutt Carey, who first heard Armstrong around 1915, said that he "played

27 Anderson, *Original Hot Five Recordings*, 240; see also Ramsey and Smith, *Jazzmen*, 12; Robert S. Gold, *Jazz Talk* (Indianapolis: Bobbs-Merrill, 1975), 116.

more blues than I ever heard in my life," even though Carey considered himself the "Blues King" at the time. "It never did strike my mind that blues could be interpreted so many different ways."[28] Listening to Armstrong's blues accompaniments from the 1920s, one occasionally senses a profound restlessness, as if the idiom can't contain all he wants to express. This restlessness becomes especially acute on the first blues recordings Armstrong made after his return to Chicago in 1925. His pianist on these sessions was usually Richard M. Jones, who takes an extremely spartan view of the pianist's role, clunking out mostly quarter-note triads in the middle register and banishing all but the most essential harmonies. On many recordings with Jones we hear Armstrong desperately flitting about, trying to eke out some scrap of interest in the austere landscape.

For variety Armstrong might have transplanted the arpeggios and high notes of his hot breaks to two-measure blues fills, but he rarely did. Nor could he rely on the organizing principle of melodic paraphrase, since blues melodies were so often fragmentary and nondescript. Armstrong had to find an alternate way of playing the blues that could sustain interest at a slow tempo and preserve the aesthetic of expressive communication that connects blues performers to their audiences. His solution was to add other harmonic resources—mostly extensions of the triad—to his gutbucket foundation, introducing a quality in his playing more characteristic of sweet music than of the blues he had known growing up.[29] As in the domains of melody and rhythm, Armstrong's rich harmonies began as isolated formulas and became more fully integrated into his language over time.

I should acknowledge at this point that, in general, critics have minimized Armstrong's contributions to jazz harmony. Collier observes that "although Armstrong frequently prepares a figure from a half-step below, he does not otherwise stray far from the chord changes. It is a mistake, I think, to give Armstrong credit for much harmonic invention."[30] Schuller concurs:

> Armstrong rarely explored new harmonic territories, but was, apparently, content to stay within the established harmonic norms of his time. Indeed, if Armstrong by chance found himself involved with a harmonically advanced or adventurous tune, it was his tendency to

---

28 Shapiro and Hentoff, *Hear Me Talkin' to Ya*, 46.

29 See Schuller, *The Swing Era*, 82, for a discussion of Duke Ellington's combination of blue notes and triadic extensions in *Reminiscing in Tempo* (1935)—"the first [Ellington] composition where these tendencies are given free rein over a prolonged period of time."

30 Collier, *Louis Armstrong*, 178.

simplify, to clarify the changes, to bring such roving harmonies under one simpler melodic/harmonic common denominator.[31]

Many examples from Armstrong's recordings on medium- to up-tempo tunes—such as "Big Butter and Egg Man" and "Potato Head Blues"—support this position. But on blues tunes, in which the tempo and the harmonic rhythm are much slower, the issue of Armstrong's harmonies becomes more complicated.

From his earliest recordings, Armstrong seems concerned to exploit conventional blues harmonies to the fullest. His first recorded solo, on "Chimes Blues," shows an unusual fidelity to the underlying progression (example 1.4). In fact, as we have seen, he makes little use of blue notes, preferring instead to outline the changing harmonies with straightforward arpeggios. As the "Chimes Blues" solo might suggest, Armstrong made frequent use of the optional passing chords played by blues pianists, banjoists, and guitarists—unlike most horn players of the period. Example 5.1 shows three blues progressions as transcribed from 1920s recordings; passing harmonies are indicated by horizontal brackets.[32] Passing chords were normally improvised and would often vary slightly from one piece to another (and even from one chorus to another), providing a fair degree of harmonic diversity in the blues repertory. Of the passing harmonies shown, Armstrong favored those occurring in the sixth, eighth, and eleventh bars. Indeed, he made them (and their variants) part of his own blues conception to the point of featuring them routinely in his own solos, even when the accompanying instrument left them out. Schuller praises Armstrong for this harmonic awareness on "Chimes Blues," while taking his fellow musicians to task: "It is worth noting...that only in Armstrong's two [solo] choruses is the harmonic change in the sixth bar performed correctly. Louis moves to an F sharp diminished chord, where previously the ensemble had stubbornly tried an F minor chord, with pianist Lil Hardin blithely continuing in F *major*!"[33]

---

31 Schuller, *The Swing Era*, 177.

32 "Camp Meeting Blues" was transcribed by Mark Tucker; "Texas Moaner" and "Weary City" by Gunther Schuller. See Mark Tucker, *Ellington: The Early Years* (Urbana: University of Illinois Press, 1991), 237; Schuller, *Early Jazz*, 96, 200.

33 Schuller, *Early Jazz*, 83. As example 5.1 shows, minor and major triads are as valid as a diminished triad in the sixth bar of a blues progression. Even if Schuller's criticism of the Creole Jazz Band members seems misplaced, though, his point about Armstrong's harmonic astuteness is apt.

EXAMPLE 5.1 Three blues progressions from the 1920s: a) "Camp Meeting Blues" (16 October 1923), Johnny Dodds's solo, King Oliver's Jazz Band; b) "Texas Moaner" (17 October 1924), Armstrong's solo, Clarence Williams's Blue Five; c) "Weary City" (1928), Johnny Dodds's solo, Johnny Dodds's Washboard Band.

(a) King Oliver's Jazz Band, "Camp Meeting Blues," 16 Oct. 1923, Johnny Dodds's solo.

(b) Clarence Williams's Blue Five, "Texas Moaner," 17 Oct. 1924, Armstrong's solo.

(c) Johnny Dodds's Washboard Band, "Weary City," 1928, Johnny Dodds's solo. Transposed for ease of comparison.

When Armstrong began accompanying blues singers, he developed the habit of playing a minor triad in the sixth bar, where the IV chord normally appeared. Sometimes he is supported by the pianist, as in the first two choruses of Ma Rainey's "See See Rider Blues" (example 5.2, no. 1). Other times he acts unilaterally, creating the impression of having made a mistake, as in the second chorus of "Reckless Blues" and in the first chorus of "You've Been a Good Ole Wagon," both with Bessie Smith. Accompanying the male singer Nolan Welsh on "St. Peter Blues," Armstrong plays a D diminished 7th chord in the sixth bar of his solo while Richard M. Jones persists with a D♭ triad (example 5.2, no. 5). Such instances (and there are many) suggest that Armstrong was pursuing his own harmonic agenda with little regard, sometimes, for his surroundings.

Occasionally the harmonic disparity between Armstrong and his accompaniment doesn't affect the quality of the performance. On 26 November 1924, Armstrong recorded a solo with the Red Onion Jazz Babies on "Terrible Blues" (example 5.3). It is an outstanding solo in conception and execution, bearing all the signs of having been honed and polished before ever gracing the recording studio. The solo is also prophetic in the harmonic subtlety of certain lines—a subtlety prized by horn players of the 1930s but well beyond the grasp of Armstrong's contemporaries. The implied passing harmonies of mm. 6 and 8 are particularly impressive. I say implied because, although the accompaniment supplies passing chords, they are not the ones Armstrong plays. While the piano and banjo play F^7, Armstrong outlines Fm^6 (m. 6), and where the accompaniment plays $C\sharp°$, Armstrong hints at $D\sharp°^7$ (m. 8). Yet these discrepancies do not clash, possibly because Armstrong plays so confidently. Nor can it be said that Armstrong aimed at the correct harmonies and missed: he is clearly on a deliberately different track. The figure in mm. 8–9, for instance, does not very well fit the chromatic bass line of the piano and banjo: $C–C\sharp°–G^7/D$. But it makes excellent sense with chromatic harmonies moving in the other direction: $C/E–D\sharp°^7–G^7/D$. In any case, he was fond of the figure and used it often—one could say habitually for a time—in the eighth bar of blues progressions. Examples appear in the fourth chorus of Maggie Jones's "Thunderstorm Blues" and the first chorus of Bessie Smith's "Sobbin' Hearted Blues" (example 5.2, nos. 2 and 3).

Armstrong appears intent on overcoming the lack of harmonic depth imposed by his one-line instrument, the cornet. His efforts wedded the function of melody and harmony in the same musical lines, creating a poignancy that would color his best blues performances in the late 1920s. The eighth bar of "Terrible Blues" seems to reveal Armstrong's determination that, if he can't play chords vertically like a piano or a

EXAMPLE 5.2   Harmonic strategies employed by Armstrong in the middle of blues progressions: 1) "See See Rider Blues" (probably 16 October 1924), first take, Ma Rainey; 2) "Thunderstorm Blues" (19 December 1924), fourth chorus, Maggie Jones; 3) "Screamin' the Blues" (17 December 1924), first chorus, Maggie Jones; 4) "Sobbin' Hearted Blues" (14 January 1925), Bessie Smith; 5) "The Bridwell Blues" (16 June 1926), Nolan Welsh; 6) "St. Peter Blues" (16 June 1926), Nolan Welsh; 7) "Have You Ever Been Down?" (6 May 1927), Sippie Wallace.

(1) Ma Rainey, "See Rider Blues," prob. 16 Oct. 1924, 1st take.

(2) Maggie Jones. "Thunderstorm Blues," 10 Dec. 1924, 4th chorus.

(3) Bessie Smith, "Sobbin' Hearted Blues," 14 Jan. 1925, 1st chorus.

(4) Nolan Welsh, "The Bridwell Blues," 16 June 1926, middle solo.

(5) Nolan Welsh, "St. Peter Blues," 16 June 1926, middle solo.

(6) Sippie Wallace, "Have You Even Been Down?" 6 May 1927, middle ensemble chorus.

EXAMPLE 5.3 Red Onion Jazz Babies, "Terrible Blues," 26 November 1924, Louis Armstrong's solo.

banjo, he will at least fit the notes in so fast horizontally that the richness of the harmony will not be lost. He could have simply run arpeggios to accomplish this end. But that would disrupt his structural melody, which in mm. 8–9 constitutes a stepwise descent from E to G. By dropping in register to supply the chord tone D♯ (as he did in m. 6 to add A♭), he could continue his melodic descent, make the line more interesting with jagged intervals, and create the illusion of accompanying himself—as if the lower chord tones were the left hand of a pianist or the strumming of a guitar.[34] And yet the lowest notes of m. 8 cannot be relegated to mere accompaniment; in some sense they play a vital harmonic role and at the

34 For a similar argument about Armstrong's singing technique, see Benjamin Givan, "Duets for One: Louis Armstrong's Vocal Recordings," *Musical Quarterly* 87 (2004): 188–218.

same time contribute to the greatest melodic beauty of the measure—possibly of the entire chorus.

In addition to adopting chromatic passing chords, Armstrong brightened the middle phrase of blues progressions (mm. 5–8) by replacing the conventional dominant seventh sonority with major sevenths and other extensions of the triad. As early as his first recording as an accompanist, on Ma Rainey's "See See Rider Blues," he featured in m. 8 of the first two choruses the major seventh of the F major triad (example 5.2, no. 1). By June 1926, he had developed a falling pattern begun on the major seventh, which appeared anywhere between mm. 5 and 8 on many recordings. On Nolan Welsh's "The Bridwell Blues" and "St. Peter Blues," Armstrong begins the pattern on the major seventh of the subdominants E♭ and D♭ respectively (example 5.2, nos. 4 and 5). Following a related impulse, perhaps, Armstrong started some months later to add ninths and elevenths to the dominant seventh chord in the ninth measure. A clear example of this practice occurs in the middle ensemble chorus of Sippie Wallace's "Have You Ever Been Down?," recorded in May 1927 (example 5.2, no. 6). The addition of the ninth and eleventh really amounts to Armstrong's substituting the ii chord, B♭ m^7, for the V chord, E♭ ^{7}, in m. 9. This substitution became standard practice on blues tunes of later jazz eras, and Armstrong's usage, which became common for him in the late 1920s, may have been one of the earliest, at least on record.

Though highlighted by moments of brilliance, many of Armstrong's blues accompaniments from 1924 to 1926 have a rough, unfinished quality to them, as if he were constantly searching for a satisfactory approach to his task. After 1926 he made only four more records as a blues accompanist, on 6 May 1927, for Sippie Wallace. By late 1927 an evident transformation had taken place: the roughness of his approach had been polished, and the restlessness replaced by a settled confidence. He was still playing gutbucket, pitch-bending, blue-note tributes to Oliver and his generation, and would continue to do so throughout his life. But another blues language had coalesced from the various harmonic ideas that emerged in his previous recordings. This language emerges full-blown in "Savoy Blues."

"SAVOY BLUES"

After making the Hot Seven recordings, Armstrong returned to the studio with his Hot Five in September and December 1927. During this period the band recorded nine sides over four sessions, including "Put 'Em Down Blues," "Ory's Creole Trombone," "The Last Time," "Struttin' with Some Barbecue," "Got No Blues," "Once in a While," "I'm Not Rough," "Hotter Than That," and "Savoy Blues," of which "Struttin'," "Hotter," and "Savoy" are the best known and most widely acclaimed. In the innovative realms of coherence, harmonic improvisation, and high-register playing, Armstrong continued to consolidate his gains, turning out a number of brilliantly conceived and executed solos. On "I'm Not Rough," "Hotter Than That," and "Savoy Blues," he expanded the group to six with the addition of guitarist Lonnie Johnson. During his duet with the regular guitarist, Johnny St. Cyr, Johnson imbued "Savoy Blues" with a quiet soulfulness that adds greatly to the mood of the piece, and is particularly effective in introducing Armstrong's solo.

That solo, while sharing some attributes with other recordings from this batch, in a larger sense stands alone. In contrast to the conventional moods of celebration ("Struttin' with Some Barbecue") or bluesy angst ("I'm Not Rough") during these sessions, Armstrong on "Savoy Blues" communicates a deep feeling of nostalgia that in hindsight becomes valedictory: this would be the last recording Armstrong made with the original Hot Five from New Orleans. The next group, meeting six months hence, would be composed almost entirely of northerners. At the same time the solo may appear to look forward, conveying a strange, anticipatory yearning. As Gene Anderson has pointed out, trombonist Kid Ory composed the piece in honor of the Savoy Ballroom, the lavish South Side dance hall that had opened just three weeks earlier, to much fanfare, on Thanksgiving eve. Armstrong would eventually become the star performer at the Savoy, but at the time of its opening he did not get the job. After many auditions and much speculation in the press, the Savoy finally hired Charles Black and Charles Elgar, two bandleaders known for their high-class entertainment. Black's orchestra was especially popular with the dancers, said Peyton, for "they are soft, sweet, and full of pep."[35] From today's vantage point, Armstrong's own sweet sounds on "Savoy Blues" shimmer with clairvoyant irony, as if forecasting that his band, in a surprising turn of events, would take Elgar's place in April of the following year, that indeed the "Savoy Blues" itself would be played at the Savoy Ballroom to a crowd "loudly wailing to Louis Armstrong for more, more, more."[36]

The power of Armstrong's solo lies primarily in the domains of rhythm and harmony (example 5.4). His "sinuous, subtle, ravishing lines, smoothly played,"[37] float along a rhythmic stream of "straight" (or even)

35 *Defender*, 7 January 1928, 6.
36 *Defender*, 5 May 1928, 7.
37 Hugues Panassié, *Louis Armstrong* (New York: Scribners, 1971; reprint, New York: Da Capo, 1980), 80.

eighth notes, eighth-note triplets, and almost rubato fluidity. Straight eighth notes, it should be emphasized, were virtually unprecedented in Armstrong's recordings. Hitherto, Armstrong seemed incapable of not swinging, but here swing (in the conventional sense) is clearly not the driving rhythmic factor. Harmonically, Armstrong presents in fully developed form some of the ideas that appeared formatively in his early blues solos and accompaniments. Significantly, he no longer emphasizes passing chords; instead he transplants their harmonic effects to the center of his lines, integrating them fully into his language. The passing harmony figure C–E–D♯–B/C–D♯–E–B at the end of m. 8 in "Terrible Blues" and "Sobbin' Hearted Blues" becomes an interior melodic module in "Savoy Blues," appearing in different guises at mm. 5, 17 (m. 5 of the second chorus), 21, even obliquely in m. 23 (example 5.5). The figure's passing function has been replaced by one of pure harmonic color, highlighting as it does the major seventh quality of the C triad.

EXAMPLE 5.4   Louis Armstrong and His Hot Five, "Savoy Blues," 13 December 1927, Louis Armstrong's solo.

The falling arpeggio in mm. 5–6 and 18 reinforces this major seventh quality and has precedents in earlier blues lines as well. In mm. 5–6 of the first two choruses of "The Bridwell Blues," Armstrong starts the figure; in mm. 5–6 of the middle solo he takes it halfway; and in mm. 4–5 of "St. Peter Blues" he completes it, all the way to the minor third below the tonic (example 5.2, nos. 4 and 5). In abstract terms the figure outlines an A minor ninth chord in "Savoy Blues," but in context it simply adds a lower thirteenth to the C major seventh chord. Armstrong shows the same interest in rich harmonies in the last third of both choruses. In mm. 9 and 21 he centers his lines around the ninth and eleventh of the chord (D^7), and he boosts the harmonic tension in m. 22 by transposing the 11–9–11–9 function of the figure in m. 9 to tonic–13–tonic–13. Clearly, in "Savoy Blues" Armstrong is using an entirely new and thoroughly integrated harmonic language, even though fragments of it had occupied his earlier blues efforts. The abundance of triadic extensions significantly enhances the emotional impact of the solo.

To explain the sudden change in style and mood on "Savoy Blues," writers have proposed various theories, including the death of Armstrong's mother earlier in the year, the advent of radio, "which required music and lyrics to be 'sweetened' for family consumption," and even halluci-nogenic drugs.[38] As suggested above, I believe that Armstrong may have been responding to a combination of musical and erotic stimuli, that he made the recording with Lombardo on the brain and romance in his heart. Let's review the timeline. Armstrong recalled hearing Lombardo "as far back as 1927." Lombardo gave his first radio broadcast in Chicago "on a cold Wednesday evening in November" of that year; Armstrong recorded "Savoy Blues" on 13 December.[39] The timing is perfect, if a bit too perfect. Is it possible that Armstrong so fully absorbed his music in the interim of just a few weeks? If Lombardo really did become the "overnight sensation" among radio listeners that his hagiographers claim (no objective historians have yet weighed in on the matter), it seems rea-sonable that the musically well-connected Armstrong would have heard about him fairly quickly. Once exposed to his music, Armstrong became a devout listener. "As long as he played [his radio broadcast] we'd sit right there," he said. "We didn't go nowhere until Lombardo signed off. That went on for months."[40] In view of Lombardo's musical simplicity and Armstrong's enthusiasm, a few weeks doesn't seem too short a time to develop an intimate familiarity with the sweet bandleader's style.

The innovations of "Savoy Blues" certainly appear related to sweet style. The triadic extensions, first of all, echo the luxuriant harmonic language employed by many sweet bands of the day. In a 1928 article titled "Jazz Is Not Music," Sigmund Spaeth praised Paul Whiteman, Vincent Lopez, and Isham Jones for developing "a 'sweet jazz' which produced soft, dreamy, subtly exotic effects, often presenting real beauty of tonal coloring."[41] Later critics, considering sweet jazz to be a commercial corruption of the real thing, saw the rich harmonies as a liability. Thus André Hodeir deni-grated sweet music in general for its "use of a sonority and a melodic and harmonic language that are exaggeratedly sugar-coated."[42] Perhaps hear-ing Lombardo prompted Armstrong to bring his rich passing chords into the body of his solos. Even more suggestive is the new rhythmic language deployed in "Savoy Blues." The flowing triplets, straight eighth notes, and rubato rhythms come straight out of the sweet expressive vocabulary.

38 Collier, *Louis Armstrong*, 187; Brooks, *Young Louis Armstrong*, 423–24.
39 Richman, *Guy*, 63.
40 Jones and Chilton, *Louis*, 130.
41 Quoted in Neil Leonard, *Jazz and the White Americans* (Chicago: University of Chicago Press, 1962), 76–77.
42 Hodeir, *Jazz*, 129–30.

The dreamy effect of these rhythms is enhanced in Lombardo's music by crooning, vocally derived ornaments: glissandi, portamenti, and brief, throwaway tremolandi. The variety in every dimension of Armstrong's playing—melodic, harmonic, and rhythmic—disguises his use of these devices, but the spirit of "Savoy Blues" exudes sweetness.

A comparison of this recording with Lombardo's "Coquette" makes this debt clear. Lombardo introduced "Coquette" during his first radio broadcast at the Granada, and his recording of this tune for Columbia on 21 March 1928 became the band's first hit.[43] Since Armstrong named "Coquette" among the early Lombardo pieces he most enjoyed,[44] it may be more than a coincidence that "Savoy Blues" shares salient features with this song. The governing motive in "Coquette" consists of an alternation between two notes a third apart, first at the tonic level (mm. 1–2: root–6–root–6, etc.), then at the dominant (mm. 3–6: root–6–root–6) (example 5.6). At both levels the colorful sixth of the chord is emphasized. Armstrong uses this same motive frequently in "Savoy Blues" (example 5.4, mm. 7, 9, 13–15, 21–22). At the beginning of his second chorus, he presents a free fantasia on the "Coquette" melody, adhering at first to the same tonic-dominant sequence, but in compressed form (mm. 13–15). Recalling from chapter 3 his ingenuity in transforming a melody, this appears to demonstrate, in reverse, the principle by which he expanded one measure of "Why Couldn't It Be Poor Little Me?" into four (example 3.2). Later in the chorus Armstrong effects a similar transformation of the same material, using his passing chord–turned–interior module to connect the tonic and dominant statements of the motive (mm. 21–22).

EXAMPLE 5.6   Guy Lombardo, "Coquette," 21 March 1928, alto saxophone melody (mm. 1–8).

43 Richman, *Guy*, 169.
44 Richman, *Guy*, 178.

The "Coquette" motive in "Savoy Blues" might appear more straight-forwardly to be a comeback of the "rocking third" stock phrase of Armstrong's apprenticeship, and it is certainly possible that old habits reinforced his usage. But Armstrong's interpretation this time is utterly different: in place of the swinging eighth notes or syncopations of the Henderson era, Armstrong here adopts the gossamer rhythms referred to above. At the beginning of the second chorus, for instance, he follows straight eighth notes with flowing eighth-note triplets and gently off-beat quarter notes—all on a rhythmic surface as calm as a placid stream. He seems to be striving for an effect similar to that of the main melody in "Coquette," which combines sustained notes, quarter-note triplets, and ties across the barline to convey a mild sense of irregular, sponta-neous vocal expression similar to the crooning of Rudy Vallee or Bing Crosby. The moment in "Savoy Blues" that sounds most like "Coquette" is undoubtedly the penultimate phrase, where Armstrong sweetens the paraphrase with half-valve glissandos swelling up to the beginning of each motive (mm. 21–22). These effects recall the slurpy lead-ins played by Carmen Lombardo, Guy's lead alto saxophonist. The second half of this phrase comes so close in rhythm and style to mm. 3–4 of "Coquette" that it sounds like a quotation. Armstrong might have been referring to these rhythmic and expressive effects when he confessed that "the Lombardos inspired us so much with their *sense of timing*... [and] their beautiful *way of phrasing*." In 1928 "we stepped right into their footsteps with our big band at the Savoy... we phrased so much like 'em until the patrons of the Savoy... all went for the 'sweetest music.'"[45]

TRANSFORMATIONS

Whatever his specific debt to Lombardo, Armstrong's co-optation of sweet style was really a transformation. When he began performing pop-ular songs with his own large orchestra in the late 1920s and early 1930s, he brought to these songs many attributes of his latest blues style. In 1930 he recorded "Sweethearts on Parade," a Lombardo tune that Armstrong admitted was a tribute to his hero.[46] And here, indeed, we find many of the triadic extensions and crooning figures that characterized "Savoy Blues." From this perspective, it may help to view Armstrong's sweet

45 Richman, *Guy.* Italics added.
46 Schuller, *The Swing Era,* 171.

manner as informing his majestic style, so plainly in evidence on the same recording. In a miracle of symbiosis, the graceful melodic undulations and soaring half-valve glissandos made the high notes more glamorous, and the high notes rendered the sweet effects more masculine. Armstrong thus became a matinee idol and a sex symbol in a way Guy Lombardo never did, despite the latter's massive record sales.

Other transformations managed to satisfy true believers in the jazz community as well. Although "Savoy Blues" does not "swing" in the manner of "Muskrat Ramble," say, no jazz fan would ever accuse Armstrong of playing squarely. Somehow, he was able to straighten out his eighth notes and lead his ideas through a fog of rubato and still sound hip. In this broader, more mystical sense, he did swing on that solo. Much as Miles Davis redefined swing through similar rhythmic heresies in the 1950s, and in the process actually enhanced his standing with the hipsters, Armstrong presented a new and more complex way of considering jazz rhythm in the 1920s. Harmonically, he enriched his vocabulary without sounding cloying or pretentious. As Lawrence Gushee writes, "Almost from the beginning, Armstrong had used such pitches [as the sixth, major seventh, and ninth] in a manner that seemed entirely natural, in distinction to such 'advanced' trumpeters as [Bix] Beiderbecke and [Red] Nichols."[47] As a result, with the exception of a few diehard New Orleans partisans, most jazz critics and fans had no problem with Armstrong's appropriations of sweet style in "Savoy Blues," which seemed to breathe the same air of knowing worldliness as his hottest excursions of the period.

This sort of discussion would have made little sense in the 1920s, when the values were reversed—that is, when sweet music was respected, and hot was suspect. Back then, "Savoy Blues" might have acquired significance mainly as a variation on the hot-sweet polarity. Ellington alluded to this variation when he recounted how trumpeter Bubber Miley changed the early sound of Ellington's band. In the summer of 1923, Ellington played with banjoist Elmer Snowden's Washingtonians at the prestigious Harlem nightclub owned by Barron Wilkins. At Barron Wilkins's, according to Ellington, the band provided soft, unobtrusive, "under-conversation music." When Miley joined the Washingtonians several months later, the band had moved to the Hollywood, a "cramped cellar" on Broadway. There, Ellington said, Miley "used to growl all night

47 Gushee, "The Improvisation of Louis Armstrong," 315.

long, playing *gutbucket* on his horn. That was when we decided to forget all about the sweet music."[48] Whereas the word *hot* evoked energetic, up-tempo jazz solos, "gutbucket" generally referred to slow, brooding statements on the blues. Miley's celebrated growling and wah-wah effects on blues pieces with Ellington epitomized the gutbucket tradition that guided Armstrong's early development as a blues player. But Ellington was exaggerating when he claimed to have forgotten about sweet music. As Mark Tucker has shown, Ellington's composition "Black and Tan Fantasy" juxtaposed gutbucket and sweet elements by following the opening minor blues section, played by Miley and trombonist Joe Nanton, with a suave, urbane second theme featuring alto saxophonist Otto Hardwick.[49] Armstrong's adoption of sweet harmonic practices on the blues created a similar gutbucket-sweet dialectic in his playing that, as we shall see in chapter 6, distinguished some of his most successful recordings in the late 1920s, including "West End Blues."

48 Tucker, *Ellington*, 89–90, 99, 101.
49 Tucker, *Ellington*, 244–45.

VERSATILITY
"WEST END BLUES"

(28 JUNE 1928)

> I wanted to do more than fake [improvise] the music all the time
> because there is more to music than just playing one style.
>
> — LOUIS ARMSTRONG

IN THE 1920S THE WATCHWORD AMONG jazz musicians hoping to make good was *versatility*. It was fine to play hot, but a band needed sweet numbers, too. There was a place for comedy, and one for virtuosity. Jazz appealed to the young dancers, but classical selections added variety and helped fill out the program. Versatility was so highly prized that some bands included the word in their name: Ely Young's Versatilians, for example, or the Versatile Five.[1] For young black musicians, especially those from New Orleans, acquiring versatility usually meant working on their "legitimate" or classical skills. A versatile orchestra, wrote Dave Peyton, is "one that is able to play 'hokum' *and* first-class music. By first-class music I mean the modern popular dance arrangements compiled by the expert arranger,

---

1   *Defender*, 25 August 1928, 6; Scott Yanow, *Classic Jazz: The Musicians and Recordings That Shaped Jazz, 1895–1933* (San Francisco: Backbeat Books, 2001), 158.

who puts it in the symphonic atmosphere." Acknowledging inherent differences between the strengths and weaknesses of black and white players, he noted that "the individuality [i.e., jazz abilities] of our musicians will be wanted in the popular field of music, and we will more than make good: *but we must have the versatility to handle the higher classes* as well as the popular music. In order to get this versatility we must perfect our sight-reading ability and our technic.... We must learn to properly command our instruments." The Charles Elgar band had struck this ideal balance: "Their dance music is red hot, and to show versatility they very artistically play the show music."[2]

For Armstrong, the quest for versatility was inextricably bound up with a parallel struggle for social respectability and status—for "class," to use the preferred term of the day. This struggle can be clearly seen in his relationships with his first three wives: Daisy Parker, Lil Hardin, and Alpha Smith. Armstrong married Daisy Parker, a New Orleans prostitute, in 1918. Their union was an unhappy one, according to Armstrong, because of Daisy's jealousy and sharp temper. His 1954 autobiography, *Satchmo: My Life in New Orleans*, recounts numerous fights in the street between Louis and Daisy, who typically hurled bricks at each other until the police intervened. One morning Louis awoke to find Daisy holding a knife to his throat.[3] When Louis moved to Chicago in 1922, Daisy stayed in New Orleans. The following year he divorced her in order to marry Lil Hardin. Around 1925 Daisy came to Chicago, apparently seeking to win Louis back. They had had little contact for several years and Daisy's temper had cooled, but Armstrong insisted that their romance was over. The "boisterous, barrel house" aspect of their relationship no longer suited his personality. "Am trying to cultivate myself," he told her.[4]

Armstrong was trying hard to satisfy the high expectations of his new wife, who occupied the opposite end of the social spectrum from Daisy. Hardin was in Armstrong's words a "high class" young woman from Memphis who had attended Fisk University and came from a family with a refined social image. Hardin's mother, who considered jazz and the blues to be morally degraded, strongly disapproved of her rough

---

2 *Defender*, 27 February 1926, 6; 8 December 1928, 6; 22 December 1928, 6. Italics added. For more on versatility, see Magee, *Uncrowned King of Swing*, 6.

3 Armstrong, *Satchmo*, 150–79; Jones and Chilton, *Louis*, 59.

4 Armstrong, *Louis Armstrong in His Own Words*, 91.

and ready son-in-law from New Orleans.[5] Complicating the situation, Armstrong had brought north a young adopted relative named Clarence Miles who had been mentally impaired by a childhood accident. Lil constantly upbraided Louis and Clarence for their breaches of etiquette and propriety. She wanted to purge Armstrong's uncouth social habits and replace them with more "dignified" behavior. Lil criticized Louis for his weight, clothes, and other aspects of his appearance. She became so domineering that other musicians called Louis "Henny," for "henpecked."[6] Although desiring to please Hardin, Armstrong responded angrily to the frequent criticism. As a result, while the two shared a congenial professional relationship, their personal life was contentious.[7]

Armstrong sought refuge in the company of Alpha Smith, an adoring young fan who attended the Vendome Theater nightly and sat in the front row to gaze at him during his performances with Erskine Tate's pit orchestra. According to Armstrong, Smith was a "sweet" Chicago girl from a modest economic background. Harboring few social pretensions, Alpha and her mother were delighted to have Armstrong visit their home—so much so that before long, probably by 1927, Louis and Clarence decided to move in permanently. Living with Alpha and her mother was a great relief because they were finally free of the incessant social pressure put upon them by Lil. As Armstrong explained it, they no longer had "to put on *aires* with a certain spoon for this—and a certain fork for that."[8] To be sure, the move didn't end Armstrong's self-improvement agenda. He accumulated the trappings of upward mobility, at any rate, buying "furs and diamonds" for Alpha and expensive clothes for himself.[9] But now he was free to make his entrée into cultivated society at his own pace and in his own way.

To some extent, Armstrong's professional activities from this period parallel the dynamics of his personal life. His music shows a similar division between highbrow and lowbrow aesthetics in the mid-1920s,

---

5   Alberta Hunter said, "Lil's mother thought she [Lil] was too good for Louis." Burton Peretti, *The Creation of Jazz: Race, Music, and Culture in Urban America* (Urbana: University of Illinois Press, 1992), 69. Hardin confirmed this, admitting in 1971, "My family gave me hell for marrying Louis; they said he was almost ignorant." Michael M. Conway, "A Genius...Didn't Have to Be Taught," *Chicago Sun-Times*, July 7, 1971, 7. Clipping in Louis Armstrong vertical file, Hogan Jazz Archive.

6   Jones and Chilton, *Louis*, 109.

7   For more on Armstrong's troubled relationship with Hardin, see Jones and Chilton, *Louis*, 109–10; Collier, *Louis Armstrong*, 156–58; Bergreen, *Louis Armstrong*, 269–76.

8   Armstrong, *Louis Armstrong in His Own Words*, 97.

9   Armstrong, *Louis Armstrong in His Own Words*, 98.

and a similar reconciliation of values near the end of the decade. It is no coincidence that Lil, Armstrong's social handler, played an important role in his assimilation of what many considered to be high-class music. As we have seen in chapter 3, Hardin drilled Armstrong in classical literature and, possibly, theory. When the opportunity came to play with Erskine Tate's "symphony orchestra" at the Vendome Theater, Lil encouraged him: "You've been wanting to get the experience of playing classic and symphony music, etc.—well, here's your chance."[10] Indeed, Armstrong reveled in his experience with Tate and savored the memory to the end of his life. Tate's orchestra was a twelve-piece ensemble with strings and double-reed woodwinds as well as the brass, clarinets, and saxophones to which Armstrong was accustomed. At the Vendome, Tate's band was required to play background music for silent pictures and to provide entertainment between reels. The orchestra played light classical pieces like von Suppé's "Poet and Peasant" and Rossini's "William Tell" overtures along with jazz and popular numbers. Armstrong played solos and alternated between first and second chair. He was required not only to read music but to watch Tate, the conductor, for sudden cuts, fades, or repeats in the printed score. The pressure was great and Armstrong didn't always execute his part successfully.[11]

Nevertheless, Armstrong became so valuable as a soloist that his occasional gaffes with the ensemble were easily forgiven. Tate even persuaded him to climb out of the pit onto the stage to play his solos. Under the Vendome spotlight, Armstrong elicited an audience response foreshadowing the frenzied adulation that followed later icons of American popular music such as Frank Sinatra and Elvis Presley. Trumpeter Doc Cheatham recalled that when he first substituted for Armstrong at the Vendome, the crowd noise was deafening as he stepped into the spotlight. Then when people realized it wasn't Armstrong playing, the screaming went "right down to nothing, and I'm up there playing like a fool."[12] According to Armstrong, his biggest feature was the Intermezzo from Mascagni's *Cavalleria Rusticana*. Later, at the Metropolitan Theater, he worked out a solo to Puccini's *Madame Butterfly*.[13] This kind of playing was unlike

10 Armstrong, *Louis Armstrong in His Own Words*, 95.
11 He once told of an incident in which he became so engrossed in the movie playing on the screen behind him that he failed to make an important entrance, causing mayhem in the rest of the orchestra. Louis Armstrong, Voice of America interview, probably July 1956, archive reel 93–001.10, Louis Armstrong Archive.
12 Giddins, *Satchmo*, 85.
13 Bergreen, *Louis Armstrong*, 266; cf. 294.

anything he had done with King Oliver or Fletcher Henderson, and Armstrong took great pride in his accomplishment. Although he rarely performed from the classical repertory in his post-1920s career, he used the Mascagni Intermezzo as a warm-up before going on stage for many years afterward.

Armstrong's engagements at the Dreamland Café, the Sunset Café, and the Savoy Ballroom filled out the education in "high-class" music he was receiving at the Vendome and Metropolitan. Both the Dreamland and the Sunset cultivated a glamorous public image. The Sunset, charging high prices and catering mostly to whites, developed an especially exclusive reputation. The house band, Carroll Dickerson's Orchestra, played floor shows with arrangements by Dave Peyton, and accompanied Charleston dancing contests. The second trumpet player, Natty Dominique, recalled that Dickerson's band played "hard music." It even performed classical pieces, including excerpts from Wagner's *Tannhäuser*.[14] Bud Freeman recalled, in a similar vein, that at the Savoy Ballroom Armstrong played Liszt's *Liebestraum*.[15] Jazz at the Sunset and the Savoy was of the high-class variety exemplified by Fletcher Henderson, featuring zany novelty solos and clever, elaborate arrangements. Moreover, as we have seen, Armstrong and his colleagues admired Guy Lombardo and sought to emulate the sweet music he played.

From 1925 to early 1928, then, Armstrong exhibited a split musical personality: in the theaters and cabarets he played operatic melodies, show music, and society jazz, while in the recording studio he played polyphonic New Orleans jazz—a rough, casual, and disreputable music compared with his evening repertory. This ability to compartmentalize, to adapt to his musical environment, was what Peyton meant by versatility. But Armstrong did not stop there. Toward the end of the Hot Five series, the two strains in his playing—high and low—began to merge. The fusion was conspicuously signaled by the sudden "northern" presence in the personnel of Armstrong's final edition of the Hot Five, but the change in his own playing occurred more gradually. By the end of the series, Armstrong had transcended mere versatility to achieve a hybridity that helped to change jazz. William Howland Kenney argues that Armstrong represented "the single, most outstanding contribution

14 Bill Russell, *New Orleans Style*, comp. and ed. Barry Martyn and Mike Hazeldine (New Orleans: Jazzology Press, 1994), 148.
15 Freeman, "The Father and His Flock," 17.

to the ongoing synthesis that produced jazz in Chicago during the twenties," fusing "African-American folk music traditions, elements of cabaret musical entertainment, and techniques borrowed from Anglo-American musical culture" (by which Kenney apparently means European concert music).[16] Nowhere is the power of this hybridity better demonstrated than in "West End Blues," the most famous and, perhaps, the most influential recording of Armstrong's career. Unlike the other developments surveyed in this book, which tended to be individual projects pertaining mostly to Armstrong's trumpet solos, his embrace of high-class musical elements was a more holistic endeavor involving his performing repertory and his entire band. Accordingly, in this chapter I discuss not only his trumpet style but also his singing, his ensemble, and the pieces he played.

AN ATTEMPTED COUP

"West End Blues" takes on new meaning in light of events leading up to it, in which Armstrong taught Dave Peyton a lesson on the limits of versatility in the conventional sense. During the first part of 1928, Peyton, one of the most powerful figures in the South Side musical community, tried to knock Armstrong off his throne as the oft-proclaimed "jazz cornet king." Peyton had been a close acquaintance of Armstrong's and, in general, an enthusiastic promoter of his work. Shortly after Armstrong returned to Chicago in 1925, Peyton declared him "the greatest jazz cornet player in the country," an assessment he repeated regularly thereafter. But in the fall of 1927 a series of interlocking events created an economic crisis for dance and cabaret musicians in Chicago. During this period Armstrong reached the low point of his career, and Peyton saw financial advantage in abandoning him. Using his editorial platform at the *Defender* and his conductor's podium at the most prestigious theater in town, Peyton tried to install a rival trumpeter in Armstrong's place of honor in the minds of the public. The coup was unsuccessful, largely because Armstrong changed the rules of a game that Peyton thought he knew cold.

In 1927 a combination of forces brought hard times to cabaret and theater musicians alike.[17] Under pressure from social reformers, federal agents began squeezing nightclubs that violated liquor laws, starting with

16 Kenney, *Chicago Jazz*, 52–60; quote on p. 58.
17 The following paragraph is indebted to William Howland Kenney's excellent discussion of this period in *Chicago Jazz*, 147–64.

a blanket raid of the South Side over Christmas, 1926. In court, club owners protested that agents were rarely able to prove alcohol sales, and that the mere possession of liquor by customers bringing their own flask was not prohibited by the Volstead Act. A series of appeals made their way to the Supreme Court, which ruled against the club owners in October 1927. Following the "hip flask ruling," the government raided dozens of cabarets, and by May over two hundred musicians had lost their jobs. These dramatic events played out against a more gradual attrition over months and years, amounting to a "slow death" of jazz-age cabarets.[18] At the same time, theater musicians were threatened by the advent of electronically produced movie soundtracks. In the summer of 1927, Vitaphone and Movietone came to Chicago theaters in the Loop district, putting 1,500 musicians out of work, and by the fall less expensive versions of this technology were crowding out live music in South Side theaters as well. Within a year, most of the leading black theater orchestras had been fired, including Erskine Tate's at the Vendome, Clarence Black's at the Metropolitan, Clarence Jones's at the Owl, and Lovie Austin's at the Monogram.

Reading between the lines of Peyton's columns, one gets the sense that he anticipated these dislocations and by the fall of 1927 had begun taking steps to ensure his professional future. For years he had admired a new system of theater entertainment pioneered by white bandleader Paul Ash. Ash popularized the use of a "stage band" that performed onstage rather than in the pit. The band played special numbers and accompanied dancing and other vaudeville acts. Throughout, Ash acted as an entertaining master of ceremonies, introducing acts, telling jokes, and kibitzing with the audience. Under this system, Ash had made the McVickers and Oriental theaters the most profitable in white Chicago. In 1927 the owners of these same theaters planned an ambitious project in the heart of the Black Belt: an entertainment complex housing a department store, a deluxe ballroom, and a fabulous new theater. The ballroom would be named the Savoy and the theater the Regal. As its name suggested, the Regal Theater was magnificent—"the largest, the most technologically advanced, and the most architecturally ornate movie house" on the South Side, and the equal of many of the finest white theaters.[19] The white corporate heads hired Stanley

18 Kenney, *Chicago Jazz*, 148.
19 Clovis E. Semmes, *The Regal Theater and Black Culture* (New York: Palgrave Macmillan, 2006), 15.

"Fess" Williams, star of the Harlem Savoy Ballroom, to serve as emcee on the Paul Ash model, and Dave Peyton to be the musical director and orchestra conductor. Peyton was given carte blanche to hire the best musicians he could find.

Peyton pursued various machinations to succeed in his new venture. In early 1928 he shamelessly promoted his interests in the *Defender* and moved against former friends and allies. "This mammoth theater will be an innovation in the community," he predicted. "Its drawing powers will have no limit so stupendous are the programs planned by the management." As for the featured attraction, Fess Williams, "he will be the shining light of the performance.... He will be the one in front bowing to the thunderous applause...of the howling audience." Peyton recruited vigorously from the Vendome orchestra, but to his disappointment only succeeded in hiring trumpeter Reuben Reeves, flutist Orville Morton, and woodwind player Charles Harris, because they had "refused to sign a contract" with Tate. "Good musicians do not have to sign contracts... with leaders," he wrote angrily. "If you have real ability, keep yourself open. You cannot tell when a greater opportunity will present itself."[20] After weeks of fevered copy, the Regal opened on 4 February to a respectable but less than overwhelming reception. Two weeks later, Peyton wrote with a touch of panic: "Chicago is beginning to like Fess Williams real well. He has grown on the folks out this way. They have learned to understand Fess better.... All the knockers, mostly musicians who are jealous of this newcomer in their midst, might as well take low." Incensed by the "knockers," Peyton advised his readers that he had "decided to blacklist the knocking brothers. This should be taken into consideration by all of the leaders and contractors."[21]

Given his talent and popularity, Armstrong would have been a natural choice for star trumpet soloist at the Regal. He had done lengthy stints at the Vendome and Metropolitan theaters, garnering effusive praise from Peyton himself. Furthermore, Armstrong was available at the time—more than available, he was unemployed, out of money, and heavily in debt. Sometime in the fall of 1927 he had left his job at the

---

20 With barely concealed schadenfreude, Peyton later wrote about Tate's trouble keeping his orchestra staffed: "Erskine Tate's Vendome theater orchestra has been supplemented by several musicians brought here from New York. The rumor is current that they are to return to the eastern city after playing three weeks at the Vendome." *Defender*, 25 February 1928, 6.

21 *Defender*, 7 January 1928, 6; 21 January 1928, 6; 14 January 1928, 6; 25 February 1928, 6; 18 February 1928, 6; 11 February 1928, 6.

Sunset Café as well as his orchestra position at the Metropolitan Theater. Together with pianist Earl Hines and drummer Zutty Singleton, he had opened his own club, the Usonia, in Warwick Hall in December. Unfortunately, the opening coincided with that of the Savoy Ballroom, a state-of-the-art enterprise, and the Usonia couldn't compete. "I don't know what happened," said Hines, "but we like to starve to death, making a dollar or a dollar-and-a-half apiece a night."[22] Cutting their losses, Armstrong and his partners pulled out of the lease, whereupon the owners promptly sued for the remaining $1,900. To make matters worse, Armstrong's new car was stolen, then returned in cannibalized form. "Earl, Zutty, and I stayed out of work so long until it was impossible for me to get my car out of the shop, even after it was fixed," Armstrong recalled. "Things gotten so tough with us until fifteen cents looked like fifteen dollars."[23] But despite Armstrong's manifest availability, Peyton had no interest in him. "There is no excuse for musicians who work all the time being broke," he wrote contemptuously, and (one strongly suspects) with Armstrong in mind. "I am speaking of the limelight popular musicians, the high-hatters who most of the time like the notoriety stuff. Be careful bunch, be careful."[24]

Peyton had in mind a different kind of player for the Regal, one who validated his bias toward classical performance values. When Armstrong had stepped down the previous year from his solo position in Erskine Tate's Orchestra at the Vendome, he was replaced by a young player named Reuben Reeves (1905–55). Originally from Evansville, Indiana, Reeves was classically trained on the trumpet, even completing a master's degree from the American Conservatory of Music. As a jazz player he imitated Armstrong, capturing the letter but not the spirit of his style, according to William Howland Kenney: "Reeves's version of Armstrong's 'shake' becomes a horse-like whinny, while falsetto vocals communicate the comical, ever so slightly condescending attitude which educated musicians often brought" to jazz.[25] According to Doc Cheatham, Reeves had a following: "Reuben Reeves went away and when he returned, they had banners on all the cars…on the South Side, at that time, welcoming Reuben Reeves back to Chicago. And they had a big display and a lot of bally-hoo about Reuben Reeves." With plenty of fire in the belly, Reeves

22 Bergreen, *Louis Armstrong*, 299.
23 Armstrong, *Louis Armstrong in His Own Words*, 99.
24 *Defender*, 3 March 1928, 6.
25 Kenney, *Chicago Jazz*, 138.

yearned to humble his model. "I don't think Reuben cared too much for Louie Armstrong's popularity," recalled Cheatham.[26]

After hiring Reeves at the Regal, Peyton did his best to help him eclipse Armstrong. His own first reviews of Reeves in early 1927 had been complimentary but measured. But when it became personally advantageous to promote him more heartily, Peyton did not hold back. A week after the Regal opened, he wrote a glowing review, emphasizing Reeves's classical credentials with words like *finished*, *clear*, *definite*, and *artistically*. His final line was nothing less than a shot across the bow aimed directly at Armstrong:

> Reuben Reeves, the cornetist, has taken Chicago by storm. He is in a class by himself. Not only a jazz artist is he, but a finished trumpeter. He is in Fess Williams' band at the Regal theater. His jazz playing is distinctly individual. His tones are clear and definite as a bell lick. He jazzes artistically and his work is void of blasty, sloppy tones that are sickening to listen to. Chicago has gone wild over Reuben Reeves, *the hottest trumpeter yet to hit the Windy City.*[27]

Three weeks later, Peyton praised Reeves even more effusively in a 360-word encomium, many times the length of his longest Armstrong review. Beginning with a paragraph of biographical material, Peyton then described his playing in the same vein as before, stressing Reeves's "unlimited versatility" and his ability to play "correctly," to "hold the first chair in the symphony orchestra and immediately transform himself into a jazz maestro." "Reuben Reeves has taken the edge on any of the jazz artists of the past," Peyton gushed. "In Chicago he is lauded the king of them all, and he is. When Reuben Reeves plays his cornet, and when he really gets happy, cold chills run up and down your spine." In an obvious dig at the untutored Oliver and Armstrong, he wrote that Reeves's "style is artistic; none of that sloppy, mushy, discordant playing that so many of our so-called jazz kings indulge in, due to the fact that they don't know their instruments theoretically." Finally, he closed by making a prediction that would actually come true—but with respect to Armstrong rather than Reeves: "If he ever goes to Broadway with his style and ability to deliver, his fortune will be made."[28]

26 Cheatham interview.
27 *Defender*, 11 February 1928, 7.
28 *Defender*, 3 March 1928, 6.

As it turned out, most of Peyton's other lofty predictions fell flat as well. Although the Regal Theater would go on to a lengthy and distinguished career, the initial plan of Paul Ash–style entertainment proved unsuccessful. Within a year the stage-band policy was discontinued and Fess Williams returned to New York.[29] For his part, Armstrong finally got back on his feet when he joined Carroll Dickerson's band at the Savoy Ballroom in April 1928. At the Savoy, Armstrong enjoyed the greatest success of his career to that point, forcing Peyton to stop flacking for Reeves and accept reality. In June Peyton turned his allegiance back to Armstrong, ostentatiously calling him "the great king Menelick," after the Ethiopian king who drove out the Italians in the nineteenth century, unsubtly noting Armstrong's superiority, regardless of race. In July he portrayed himself, with remarkable chutzpah, as Armstrong's close friend and mentor: "One of my most valued friends is King Menelik, who is none other than the great Louis Armstrong, the jazz cornet wizard, who has slaughtered all of the ofay [white] jazz demons appearing at the Savoy recently. Louis doesn't get 'hot' until this writer gives him a look and yells, 'Go get him, Louie,' and then the war is on." Meanwhile, silence on Reuben Reeves. While on vacation Armstrong shrewdly sent Peyton a postcard, and Peyton responded in kind, publishing a glowing report of his return, and closing with his formerly held opinion: "Mr. Menilick [sic] has no peer anywhere in the world when it comes to jazz cornet playing." By contrast, when Reeves returned from *his* vacation the next month, Peyton wrote only two lines: "Reuben Reeves, cornetist in the Regal theater orchestra, has returned from his vacation. He motored to Evansville, Ind., visiting his people."[30]

Still, old ways of thinking die hard. In what must have felt like a moment of real vindication, Armstrong was booked the following year for a week's run at the Regal Theater, beginning 28 April. It may have been during this engagement that Armstrong and Reeves joined horns in a decisive contest. Previewing the event, Peyton praised Armstrong (referring to himself in the third person): "He has been in rehearsal for the past week with Dave Peyton, musical director of the Regal, and what is to be presented by Louis is just 'too hot.'" But at the theater Peyton and Reeves plotted an ambush, according to Danny Barker, who in time-honored jazz tradition heard the story secondhand:

29 Semmes, *The Regal Theater*, 41; Kenney, *Chicago Jazz*, 157–58.
30 *Defender*, 14 July 1928, 6; 4 August 1928, 6; 11 August 1928, 6; 8 September 1928, 6.

Before the show started, the house orchestra...always played a long five- to eight-minute overture, usually a classical or sedate piece of music. But Mr. Peyton scored up an arrangement real hot and frantic this time, featuring Mr. Reuben Reeves blowing his utmost, playing every technique and trick he knew. Blowing like this before Louis Armstrong was to appear on stage was a secret move designed to embarrass Louis; it was deliberate and most impolite—I'd say it was vicious....

Louis heard the frantic screaming wailing horn and, as the story goes, he left his dressing room in his robe and peeped through the curtains down at the orchestra and watched as Mr. Peyton dramatically directed Mr. Reeves by flailing his arms while Mr. Reeves screamed to the high heavens, trying to blow the roof off the Regal Theater....

When the stage manager knocked on Louis's dressing-room door telling him it was time to appear, Louis picked up his horn, walked onto the stage to a tremendous ovation, and bowed and smiled, glancing first at Peyton and then at Reeves. The eyewitness says that Louis blew one or two hundred choruses of *Chinatown* (or *Tiger Rag*). The audience was completely spellbound; they had never heard horn playing like that. They just sat there, electrified, and Reeves and Peyton sat petrified. I forgot to ask the eyewitness if Dave Peyton changed the overture to something less fiery.[31]

It may be that this incident occurred in early 1928, when Peyton and Reeves seemed most primed for a confrontation. Or perhaps the anecdote is apocryphal. Whatever the case, the story bears witness, in all likelihood, to a genuine perception: either in actual or symbolic combat, Armstrong roundly defeated another jazz trumpeter with classical training and a master's degree. The widespread notion that such training made a big difference was laid to rest along with Reeves's dreams of dominance.

MOVING TOWARD URBANITY

It would be misleading to view Armstrong's defeat of Reeves as a triumph of jazz over classical performance values. For one thing, according to Barker's account, Reeves challenged Armstrong as a jazz player, "screaming" and "wailing" to a "hot and frantic" accompaniment. For

---

31 Barker, *A Life in Jazz*, 129–30.

another, if Armstrong's recordings are any indication, he had grown considerably in his standard technique—his classical chops, so to speak—between 1927 and 1929. As Zutty Singleton recalled, Reeves "was pushing Louis there for a time."[32] One can envision Armstrong bearing down on his studies under the pressure he felt from Reeves and Peyton. He must have practiced hard, because the next batch of Hot Fives, in June 1928, shows a noticeable change. Armstrong's tone, always gorgeous, is even more brilliant and controlled; his high notes more resonant; his execution more assured. His victory over Reeves probably reflected not only his preeminence as a jazz player but also his ability to hold his own as a trumpet player. As Peyton admitted in previewing Armstrong's Regal appearance, "Louis is famed as an eccentric cornetist. Then, too, he is quite a legitimate artist, having great command over his instrument."[33]

For Armstrong, this move toward urbanity represented a broad-based campaign involving his band and repertory in addition to his own playing. Through 1927 he had contracted primarily New Orleanians, most of them old friends, to play on the Hot Five records: Johnny Dodds, Baby Dodds, Kid Ory, Johnny St. Cyr, Lonnie Johnson. When he returned to the studio in June 1928, however, he made an about-face. With the exception of drummer Zutty Singleton, Armstrong surrounded himself with northern musicians, all of whom played with him in Carroll Dickerson's band at the Savoy Ballroom: Jimmy Strong (clarinet, tenor saxophone), Fred Robinson (trombone), Earl Hines (piano), and Mancy Carr (banjo). Armstrong considered the Chicago Hot Five, as I call this band, "one of the Damnedest bands there were."[34] With this band Armstrong made a profound impression at the Savoy. "When he gets through with his cyclonic jazz figures," Peyton writes, "he stops the ball. Louis is the only musician I know of who really stops the ball, just as an actor stops a show."[35] Although Armstrong had received adulation before, his tenure at the Savoy generated a mass following that would only increase over the years. In the summer of 1928 he renegotiated his contract for $200 a week, more than three times the scale salary of a regular working musician ($65) and $50 more than the top salary quoted by Peyton.[36] With

32 Jazz Oral History Project, interview with Zutty and Marge Singleton, by Stanley Dance, Institute of Jazz Studies.
33 *Defender*, 27 April 1929, 6.
34 Armstrong, *Louis Armstrong in His Own Words*, 101.
35 *Defender*, 28 April 1928, 6.
36 Ramsey and Smith, *Jazzmen*, 137; *Defender*, 1 October 1927, 6; 24 December 1927, 6.

success opening up to him, the time had come to consolidate his efforts and use some of the same musicians for both live and recorded performances.

The personnel shake-up may have been sudden, but the changes in Armstrong's music came more gradually. One can discern occasional "northern" infiltrations into the recordings of the original Hot Five. Most of the tunes from the first batch of Hot Five recordings exhibit an informal, lighthearted quality typical of New Orleans musical practice. Their titles often evoke southern rural images: "Gut Bucket Blues," "Georgia Grind," "Muskrat Ramble," "Droppin' Shucks," "King of the Zulus," "Big Fat Ma and Skinny Pa." At the end of 1926, though, Armstrong foreshadowed the Chicago Hot Five with four pieces he performed at the Sunset Café, two of which feature singer Mae Alix. Armstrong composed the pieces in collaboration with Percy Venable, the producer of the floor shows at the Sunset. In contrast to earlier Hot Five recordings, these titles reflect a northern urban environment: "Big Butter and Egg Man," "Sunset Cafe Stomp," "You Made Me Love You," and "Irish Black Bottom." One of these, "You Made Me Love You," gets appropriately high-class treatment with an arranged introduction. Armstrong opens the piece with an ascending scale in straight eighth notes, staccato; then after a slight ritardando the ensemble joins him on a sustained augmented dominant triad. Formal and dramatic, this is the sort of introduction that might have opened a number in a floor show. As Ory's halting, ragged entrance suggests, it was also the sort that appeared rarely in New Orleans jazz ensembles. Almost a year passed before the band used a similar introduction.

In the last batch of New Orleans Hot Fives, recorded in late 1927, society elements begin popping up more frequently, probably in connection with his open embrace of sweet style on "Savoy Blues," discussed in chapter 5. "The Last Time" opens with Dodds playing a swung eighth-note line that ends on a sustained dominant seventh chord in the ensemble. Three months later the band employs more devices from the nightclub environment. On "Once in a While" the horns twice fill breaks with a sustained, closely voiced dominant seventh chord (minus the fifth), arriving on beat two of the first bar. And during Armstrong's stop-time solo the band replaces the simple accompaniments of previous tunes (e.g., beat one of every two measures in "Potato Head Blues") with a more involved pattern: the secondary rag rhythmic grouping, three plus three plus two, taken from the melody. Originated by ragtime pianists, this pattern also appears in the music of arranged bands like those of Henderson and Ellington. As Mark Tucker has written, Ellington used it in "Down in Our Alley Blues" "to make a 'trick' introduction, as the stuttering effect momentarily obscures the metric flow."[37] In "Once in a While" Ory again has trouble executing the rhythm and "steps in a hole," as jazz musicians would put it, by playing during a rest in the second sixteen measures of Armstrong's chorus.

Six months later, Armstrong dramatically accelerated his assimilation of highbrow musical characteristics. The Chicago Hot Five recorded nineteen pieces, including the duet on "Weatherbird" by Armstrong and Hines. The recordings were made in two roughly equal groups spaced six months apart—the first nine on 27, 28, and 29 June and 5 July 1928, and the last ten on 4, 5, 7, and 12 December. New Orleans elements faded gradually in the Chicago Hot Five. Whereas on the summer recordings certain traits from the original Hot Five still persisted, by December the band's style was often indistinguishable from that of Henderson or Ellington.

Society features in the Chicago Hot Five appear in the domains of instrumentation, repertory, texture, harmony, form, and interpretation. The first and most important shift in instrumentation had already occurred when Armstrong took up the trumpet, a development reviewed in chapter 4. Earl Hines also switched to a more highbrow instrument, at least temporarily, when he played the celeste on "Basin Street Blues." The delicate tinkling of the celeste evoked the world of classical music as well as the glittering ambiance of the black-and-tans. Drummer Zutty Singleton brought stylish sound effects to the band as well. His equipment may not have originated in the symphony, but with it he created clever and humorous effects prized on the nightclub scene. He could make a sound like horse's hooves, as in his accompaniment to the trombone solo on "West End Blues," or he could imitate a tap dancer, as in his breaks during the introduction to "Sugar Foot Strut." On three pieces Singleton used brushes to suggest a whispering elegance. Finally, Armstrong added a second reed player, Don Redman, at the end of the series on "No One Else but You," "Beau Koo Jack," "Save It Pretty Mama," "Hear Me Talkin' to Ya," "St. James Infirmary," and "Tight Like This." The addition made possible a number of sonorous combinations never used by the original Hot Five: alto plus tenor saxophone or either one plus clarinet—along with the trumpet and trombone already available.

The expanded instrumentation allowed the band to play more involved arrangements. Armstrong hired Redman partly for his playing skill, but mostly for his reputation as a top-notch arranger. Redman

---

37 Tucker, *Ellington: The Early Years,* 226.

arranged Henderson's music for years, and before joining Armstrong had most recently been the leader and arranger of McKinney's Cotton Pickers, the house band at the Graystone Ballroom in Detroit.[38] Armstrong needed an arranger because his repertory had changed substantially during the past year. Out of nine pieces recorded in late 1927, six were composed by members of the band and had a strong New Orleans or blues flavor: "Ory's Creole Trombone," "Struttin' with Some Barbecue," "Got No Blues," "I'm Not Rough," "Hotter Than That," and "Savoy Blues." The other three, "Put 'Em Down Blues," "The Last Time," and "Once in a While" were Tin Pan Alley songs written by outsiders, even though after Armstrong's vocals the band played them in polyphonic New Orleans fashion. By 1928 this relationship was reversed: out of nineteen recordings only "West End Blues," "No (Papa, No)," "Weatherbird," and "Muggles" were outright blues or New Orleans tunes. Now some of the popular song-type numbers were written by Armstrong, Hardin, or Hines. Armstrong's "Hear Me Talkin' to Ya," for instance, sounds like a showpiece for a nightclub production number and bears little resemblance—in form, texture, or mood—to the rough-and-tumble "Potato Head Blues"-style vehicles of yore. Armstrong needed the services of Redman and other arrangers because his music now demanded precise synchronization of parts, as well as ingenious orchestrations of the band's newly expanded and enriched instrumental palette.

Arranged characteristics in the Chicago Hot Five can best be understood in terms of texture. Polyphonic ensembles on the opening melody or outchorus continued to play an important role, appearing in all the medium- and up-tempo pieces from the summer of 1928: "Fireworks," "Skip the Gutter," "A Monday Date," "Don't Jive Me," "Sugar Foot Strut," "Two Deuces" (double-time section), and "Knee Drops." As in the original Hot Fives, homophonic introductions and interludes represent the first incursions on traditional New Orleans texture, and also show up in these seven tunes. The introduction to "Don't Jive Me" presents a rapid succession of triplet chords played by the three horns, again reflecting the ostentatious, polished character of openings to floor shows. The introduction is impressive not only for its purely musical effect, but also for its difficulty: it is hard to imagine Johnny Dodds or Kid Ory tonguing so quickly and cleanly.

By December such unified precision characterized the ensembles, too. "No One Else but You," "Beau Koo Jack," and "Hear Me Talkin' to Ya" all

---

38 Armstrong, Voice of America interview, part 4, archive reel 93–001.12, Louis Armstrong Archives.

jettison the New Orleans polyphonic style in favor of tightly executed homophony. Particularly telling is the outchorus on "Beau Koo Jack," an Alex Hill arrangement listing Armstrong as cocomposer. Armstrong's lines soar like those of the hottest outchoruses of the original Hot Five, but his leaping, jagged rhythms aren't complemented by the unpredictable cries of an Ory or a Dodds playing under him. Instead, every step is planned in advance, every rhythm reinforced by the other horns or cast against a backdrop of sustained chords. The result is an odd cross between rousing New Orleans polyphony and the later homophonic shout choruses of the swing era. Although Armstrong seems to be improvising at times, that impression is neutralized by his sidemen's accompaniment, clearly dictated by Hill and impeccably tailored to Armstrong's lines.

The Chicago Hot Five fashioned an intriguing variety of textures in keeping with the northern preoccupation with constant surprise, novelty, and originality. The band found especially inventive ways to vary the texture of solo with rhythm section accompaniment. On "Save It, Pretty Mama," Armstrong plays a filigreed version of the melody with a straight mute (or else at some distance from the microphone) while Jimmy Strong plays ascending half notes in the low, chalumeau register of the clarinet. The very idea departs from the practice of the original Hot Five, which exploited two basic textures: the full ensemble and the soloist (with or without rhythm section). In "Save It, Pretty Mama," the instrumental juxtaposition plays off the contrasting timbres and rhythmic speeds and inverts the conventional New Orleans relationship of clarinet above the trumpet. The trumpet and clarinet create a "pretty opening mood," in the words of Schuller, "in character not unlike that of Ellington's [later] 'Mood Indigo,'"[39] another piece that placed instruments in unusual registers relative to one another.

Pianist Earl Hines contributed some of the most striking accompanimental textures. He achieved sophisticated effects by playing in extreme registers or by using "bottom-heavy" tremolos, as Jeffrey Taylor perceptively notes, to affect the sound of a parlor organ (as on "Two Deuces").[40] A more complex texture occurs in "No (Papa, No)." Here, as Armstrong embellishes the opening blues melody, Hines sympathetically echoes his ideas in treble octaves, leaving his left hand out of the picture. According to Taylor, treble octaves were a hallmark of Hines's so-called trumpet-style piano, and this example certainly supports that notion. Reaching

39 Schuller, *Early Jazz*, 129.
40 Jeffrey Taylor, "Earl Hines and Black Jazz Piano in Chicago, 1923–28" (PhD diss., University of Michigan, 1993), 148.

far beyond his traditional accompanimental role, Hines turns the chorus into a virtual duet. Yet by keeping ideas brief and simple, he still manages to sound like accompaniment rather than like a competitor for the spotlight.

In 1928 Armstrong also sought formal unpredictability in his recordings, and in this realm the Chicago Hot Five surpassed its New Orleans predecessor. Compare, for example, the straightforward formal plan of "Struttin' with Some Barbecue" with the more complex design of "Beau Koo Jack" (table 6.1).

Other pieces of the original Hot Five may have displayed more formal subtlety than "Struttin' with Some Barbecue," but none could match the intricacy of "Beau Koo Jack" or most of the other Chicago Hot Fives. Formal ingenuity did not matter to Armstrong, Ory, and Dodds, the way it did to Armstrong and Dickerson's Savoyagers. Complexity of form hinted at the musicians' classical awareness and musical sophistication. And although most nightclub patrons probably cared little about actually comprehending the musical structure, they must have delighted in the unexpected twists that popped up constantly in a piece like "Beau Koo Jack."

The Chicago Hot Five provided an ideal context for Armstrong to explore the sweet harmonies he had introduced on "Savoy Blues." The sentimental melodies to "A Monday Date," "Two Deuces," "No One Else but You," and "Hear Me Talkin' to Ya" prominently feature major and minor sevenths, as well as ninths and thirteenths in their opening phrases. Such pieces, which may have been part of Armstrong's nightly repertoire at the Savoy Ballroom, must have encouraged him to incorporate his initially blues-derived triadic extensions into his solos on popular love songs. In the fifth bar of his muted solo on "Two Deuces," for example, Armstrong ascends to the major seventh of the chord (not in the original melody) and falls down by thirds to the thirteenth below the root, just as he had fallen into the habit of doing in the fifth bar of his accompanimental blues choruses. Three measures later he lingers on the ninth of the supertonic before sinking chromatically to the augmented fifth of the dominant. The band also unveiled self-consciously "modern" harmonies, often with great fanfare. In the 1920s, society bands in theaters and fashionable nightclubs evoked an aura of worldliness and sophistication by using augmented triads, whole-tone scales, and other exotic-sounding harmonies. Whereas the original Hot Five harmonized mostly in thirds and sixths, the Chicago Hot Five sometimes deployed parallel fourths, as in the second phrase of the melody on "No One Else but You." Whole-tone harmonies appear in the ensemble break that divides the outchorus on "Beau Koo Jack."

The Chicago Hot Five contrasted with the New Orleans Hot Five by showcasing Armstrong through interpretive techniques deriving from classical music: dynamics, articulation, tempo, vibrato. Such techniques especially strengthen Armstrong's solos on "Muggles" and "Tight Like This." "Muggles" consists entirely of four solos on the twelve-bar blues: one chorus each for piano, trombone, clarinet, and two choruses for Armstrong. Hines is accompanied by Singleton swishing his brushes on the snare; Robinson and Strong receive the added punch of Hines and banjoist Mancy Carr on all four beats. Armstrong's solo is framed by an arranged background that in itself generates excitement. First, the opening eight measures of the solo are in a double-time feel—that is, the perceived beat moves twice as fast, but the harmonic rhythm stays the same. Second, the rest of the band provides a background filled with motion on four levels: the horns play whole notes (based on the original tempo); Singleton swishes his brushes on quarter notes; Cara strikes his banjo on eighth notes (the double-time tempo); and Hines plays tremolos. Above this, Strong and Robinson swell their sustained notes, playing a crescendo on the first measure, a decrescendo on the second, and so on to the eighth measure. The entire effect causes the music to sound alive, with the rhythm section providing the animation and the horns the respiration. Without this effective background Armstrong's canny rhythmic exploits would lose much of their rhetorical force.

If Armstrong's sidemen mined high-toned musical sources to better support their leader, Armstrong also did some mining of his own. His classically influenced (or aspirational) manner can be heard clearly on "Tight Like This" and "Hear Me Talkin' to Ya." "Tight Like This," with its slow oscillation between minor tonic and major dominant and its marchlike beat, distinctly evokes Spanish or flamenco music. Armstrong plays "clarion-like phrases," in the words of John Chilton,[41] repeating broad ascending fifths (E–B) and fourths (F♯–B) that share little with conventional jazz phraseology but much with the proud, martial trumpet style of Spain later exemplified by such virtuosos as Raphael Mendez. The Spanish connection becomes even more evident as Armstrong, in tempo rubato, dashes off a chromatic turn before ascending a minor arpeggio into the high register. "Hear Me Talkin' to Ya" reveals a different approach. In the second strain of the piece Armstrong plays a series of high As, then executes a brief scale passage up to high D. In keeping

41 John Chilton, liner notes to *Louis Armstrong, Volume IV: Louis Armstrong and Earl Hines*, Columbia Jazz Masterpieces, CBS Records, 1989, 45142.

TABLE 6.1 A formal comparison of "Struttin' with Some Barbecue" and "Beau Koo Jack."

Struttin' with Some Barbecue			*Beau Koo Jack*		
Intro	(12)	ensemble	Intro	(8)	ensemble/woodwinds
A	(16)	ensemble	A	(8)	ensemble
A´	(14)	banjo break	A´	(8)	
	(2)		B	(4)	alto sax break
				(4)	ensemble
A	(16)	clarinet solo	B´	(4)	alto sax break
A´	(16)	trombone solo		(4)	ensemble
A	(16)	trumpet solo	Interlude	(4)	ensemble
A´	(14)				
	(2)	clarinet/trombone: homophonic break	C	(2)	ensemble
				(2)	alto sax break
A	(14)	ensemble outchorus		(2)	ensemble
	(2)	banjo break		(2)	alto sax break
A´	(8)	ensemble outchorus	D	(6)	ensemble
				(2)	trombone break
Coda	(10)	trumpet, clarinet, trombone	C´	(2)	ensemble

	(2)	piano break
	(2)	ensemble
	(2)	piano break
D′	(8)	ensemble
C	(8)	alto sax solo (breaks every 2 bars)
D	(8)	cont. (no breaks)
C′	(8)	piano solo (breaks every 2 bars)
D′	(8)	cont. (no breaks)
C	(8)	trumpet solo (breaks every 2 bars)
D	(8)	cont. (no breaks)
C′	(8)	cont. (breaks every 2 bars)
D′	(8)	cont. (no breaks)
C	(4)	alto sax break
Coda	(30)	ensemble outchorus
	(4)	

with the "dicty" nature of the piece, this passage reflects classical beauty and restraint. The ascending even eighth notes are primly articulated and the high note is typically big and bell-like, but beautifully capped by an elegant vibrato instead of the trademark shake that so often electrifies Armstrong's high notes on hotter tunes.

This evidence of highbrow influence on the Chicago Hot Five does not mean that Armstrong had abandoned his musical roots. Most of the tunes still swing, there is plenty of blues feeling, and Armstrong himself is playing some of the most successful solos of his career. And for all the added refinement, Armstrong never took himself too seriously. On "A Monday Date" Armstrong and Hines engage in a short comic exchange that illustrates the point:

[At the beginning of the record Hines is playing unaccompanied at a fast tempo.]

ARMSTRONG: Say, say, say, say, Earl Hines! Why don't you let us in on some of that good music, Pops?

HINES: Well, c'mon here, let's get it together then.

ARMSTRONG: Well, all right—tune up, boys.

[Piano and horns play concert B♭.]

ARMSTRONG: How is that—is that all right? Is that all right?

HINES: Oh, that sounds pretty good.

ARMSTRONG [sarcastically]: Yes, that sounds pretty good. I bet if you hadn't had a half a pint of Miss Urzey's gin you wouldn't say that sounds pretty good! Well, anyhow, we gonna play anyway. Say, c'mon, Zutty, whip them cymbals, Pops!

Armstrong may have taken pride in his ability to play excerpts from the classical repertory, but he wasn't above parodying the most fundamental rite of the concert establishment: tuning up.

Armstrong saw no contradiction between his New Orleans heritage and the society music he was recording with the Chicago Hot Five. This is made clear on the opening of "Hear Me Talkin' to Ya." The arranged introduction, which sounds very chic, sophisticated, and unspontaneous, is followed by Armstrong exclaiming in his gruffest and most soulful voice: "Oh, hear me talkin' to ya!" The juxtaposition seems incongruous, but indicates how Armstrong must have felt about his situation: whatever the style of his music, he performed it with the same honest intent. Moreover, such an aesthetic and stylistic mix characterized the musical world he knew growing up. Jazz and the blues intermingled with hymns and sentimental songs in New Orleans streets, and uptown "ratty" players collaborated—however testily—with downtown classically trained musicians in various engagements around the city. Not surprisingly, Armstrong interpreted some of the society elements in his 1928 recordings as coming from New Orleans. Regarding the elegant recording of "Basin Street Blues," Armstrong said that it "explains everything you need to know about New Orleans." The understatement and refinement in the performance only prove, he continued, that "jazz can be played just as pretty as it can be played loud.... It ain't just one style." No, it ain't—as "West End Blues," another piece by this band, beautifully demonstrates.

"WEST END BLUES"

Thus far in this book, I have addressed a variety of different idioms common in popular music of the 1920s: novelty, hot, sweet, gutbucket, and classical. All of these make an appearance in "West End Blues." To make sense of them culturally as well as musically, I will borrow the concept of topic theory from Western art musicology.[42] In music of the eighteenth century, composers used characteristic figures—which Leonard G. Ratner calls "topics"—to communicate particular meanings to their audiences. Common topics included *singing style, brilliant style, learned style, French overture, Hunt music, Turkish music,* and so forth. These topics were identified and defined by eighteenth-century theorists and were presumably part of a common verbal language that composers used to discuss their music. For Ratner, topics can reveal "expressive qualities" and even "poetic implications" that may enrich the experience of a knowledgeable and sensitive listener.[43] As one might expect, the poetic implications stand out especially strongly in the context of theater. Wye Jamison Allenbrook has shown how Mozart used dance types to underscore dramatic points in *Le nozze di Figaro* and *Don Giovanni.*[44] When middlebrow Figaro addresses the Count in the style of the noble minuet, he expresses not only an uppity determination to outwit him but also the Enlightenment conviction that true nobility is a product of character and intelligence, not birth. And when the Count responds to his underlings in the style of the

---

42 For previous applications of this notion to jazz and other types of black music, see Horace J. Maxile Jr., "Say What? Topics, Signs, and Signification in African American Music" (PhD diss., Louisiana State University, 2001), and Magee, "Everybody Step," 697–732.

43 Leonard G. Ratner, *Classic Music: Expression, Form, and Style* (New York: Schirmer, 1980), 30.

44 Wye Jamison Allenbrook, *Rhythmic Gesture in Mozart: Le nozze di Figaro and Don Giovanni* (Chicago: University of Chicago Press, 1983).

pompous French overture or the military march, he seems overbearing and somewhat desperate, as if by simply flaunting the trappings of his social status he can redeem his rapidly diminishing moral authority.

Jazz topics had social meaning, too. According to the broad stereotypes of the 1920s, *hot* was associated with originality and energy, but also, potentially, with immorality, crime, black culture, and the lower classes. Likewise, *sweet* represented the opposite: white culture, decorum, refinement, and the upper classes. A musician who learned both could, like Figaro, adjust his status to fit the needs of the occasion, boost his professional reputation, and make more money. And a musician who mixed both, like Armstrong, could confound social expectations altogether. Of such confusion are classic performances often made.

Consider "West End Blues," a veritable cocktail of jazz topics that also nicely recapitulates most of the developments treated in this book (example 6.1). The piece boasts a down-home New Orleans pedigree both through authorship—it was written by King Oliver—and through the reference in the title to a "resort for Negroes" on Lake Pontchartrain, according to Oliver's wife, Stella.[45] Nevertheless, Armstrong's celebrated opening cadenza presents a restlessness of topic and tempo that only obliquely forecasts the main gutbucket disposition of the whole (mm. 1–9). His opening phrase divides into two parts that reflect back on one another. The first part combines punchy quarter notes with syncopations in a descending line that could be heard in either C minor or E♭ major (mm. 1–2). This obviously hot riff is followed by the second part of the phrase, a line of very different connotations (mm. 3–4). The devil-may-care descent becomes a martial fanfare climbing to the high register; the bouncy quarter-note swing gives way to legato eighth-note triplets in a slower tempo; and the ambiguous harmony of the opening bars is replaced by a clear exposition of C minor, as Armstrong ratchets upward through a succession of arpeggios to high C (high D to him). Just as the first part of the phrase alludes to his background as a jazz player, the second part reveals his familiarity with classical devices. Schuller writes that in this introduction, "Louis had found the perfect jazz counterpart to the hundreds of popular cornet cadenzas" performed by the likes of Herbert L. Clarke.[46] Indeed, the rising C minor arpeggios explicitly evoke this tradition: an identical pattern begins J. B. Arban's famous third "Characteristic Study" for cornet (example 6.2).

45 Wright, "Stella Oliver Talks," 106; see also Brothers, *Armstrong's New Orleans*, 223.
46 Schuller, *Early Jazz*, 115.

EXAMPLE 6.1 Louis Armstrong and His Hot Five, "West End Blues," 28 June 1928, Louis Armstrong's trumpet part. Adapted from Charles Burckhardt, with William Rothstein, *Anthology for Musical Analysis*, 6th ed. (Belmont, CA: Thompson Schirmer, 2008), 598

EXAMPLE 6.2 J. B. Arban, Characteristic Study no. 3, opening.

The classical turn serves to arouse the listener: Armstrong's sudden formal presentation infuses the initially lighthearted opening with an unexpected feeling of drama and gravity. Despite the contrast, the classical insertion doesn't seem out of place, possibly because Armstrong links the two parts structurally. They actually represent different interpretations of the same basic idea. The second part can be heard as a loose retrograde version of the first, starting with the exact backward repetition of pitches moving chromatically away from E♭, and continuing through a retracing of the C minor chord tones, only reaching past the original starting pitch G to high C. It is as if Armstrong were showing two sides of himself, sides that, despite their fundamental differences, reveal equal confidence and "authenticity." In 1928, few trumpet players could swing as effortlessly as Armstrong does in these opening measures. Even fewer, no doubt, could match his majestic ascent to the trumpet's high D. Tellingly, he does not execute that D the way he did the high Cs on "S.O.L. Blues," with lowdown rips and shakes. The power is still there, but following a clearly different objective Armstrong warms the note with beautifully controlled vibrato. In juxtaposing this passage against the opening, he seems to be saying to the Peytons of the world: "You want versatility? Dig this!"

The second phrase of the cadenza resumes the fast tempo of the opening while turning sharply toward the gutbucket mood that dominates the rest of the recording. The first half of the phrase projects the blues by dwelling on the blue notes G♭ and D♭ (mm. 5–6). As Lewis Porter has demonstrated, the last half originated in a solo Armstrong played four years earlier, on "Changeable Daddy of Mine," a blues-drenched pop song recorded by Margaret Johnson and Clarence Williams's Blue Five (mm. 7–9).[47] Together with the bluesy flavor, the irrepressibly jaunty spirit of this phrase contrasts strongly with the serious tone of the previous one, as if Armstrong were mocking himself—or, more likely, the pretensions of those who might be overawed by such a display of classical acumen. One is reminded of a similar rhetorical device in his prose writing: after using a big, pretentious word, Armstrong would often deflate it by asking, mischievously: "Did that come outa mee?"[48]

Again, Armstrong connects this topic to the previous two through motivic consistency. From the hot opening he retains the idea of two

---

47 Lewis Porter, liner notes to *Louis Armstrong and Sidney Bechet in New York, 1923–1925,* Smithsonian Recordings R026 (1981), 5.

48 Armstrong, *Louis Armstrong in His Own Words,* 115.

descending triads, each at a different pitch level; from the classical turn he keeps the ascending chromatic triplet figure. The gutbucket continuation thus consists of expanded and embellished repetitions of these elements from the opening. Armstrong begins with descending minor triads, first on E♭, then on B♭. These are followed by two ascending chromatic triplets, the first of which leads to an implied dominant seventh (D♭). He then repeats the sequence with descending F minor and C minor triads, related by a perfect fourth as before. The cadenza closes with a final ascending chromatic triplet which Armstrong again directs toward the implied dominant seventh (A♭), only an octave lower this time. The varied repetitions in the long, gradually descending third part dissipate the tension established by the classical ascent and balance the compact, emotionally charged opening.

In the first chorus after the introduction, Armstrong leads the band in a complete statement of the twelve-bar melody (mm. 11–22). Armstrong's lead begins simply, staying close to the melody and upholding the basic gutbucket temper of the piece. In the second half of the chorus, however, his lines become more elaborate and his stylistic palette broadens. In mm. 17–18 he makes reference to a sort of modified clarinet style, adding upper appoggiaturas to the standard sawtooth pattern. This is immediately followed by an open reference to sweet music (mm. 18–20). The fluid rhythms, graceful sweeping contours, and emphasis on triadic extensions create a very different mood from the hot-gutbucket manner of the piece as a whole. Deviating ever further from the melody, Armstrong presents a C minor seventh arpeggio against the underlying harmony of B♭ dominant, lingering finally on the thirteenth of the chord. At the end of the chorus he closes out his lead statement with a rising series of classical arpeggios that, as Schuller noted, is a variation of the second part of his opening cadenza (mm. 21–22).

After Armstrong's statement of the melody, he yields the spotlight to his trombonist, John Thomas, who plays a conventional but perfectly respectable gutbucket-style solo. What is interesting here is the juxtaposition of this solo with the material in the rhythm section. Pianist Earl Hines plays shimmering tremolos throughout, while drummer Zutty Singleton plays a clippety-clop accompaniment on "horse's hooves"—a novelty percussion instrument. Thus we encounter a three-tiered texture, presenting the distinct topics of gutbucket, classical, and novelty, all at the same time.

The third chorus features a call-and-response duet between clarinetist Jimmy Strong and a scat-singing Louis Armstrong (example 6.3). Given over entirely to sweet style, Armstrong's singing here has been described as "heart-warming," "beautiful and nostalgic," "tender and suave."[49] As these wistful adjectives might suggest, this chorus evokes a haunting quality similar to that of "Savoy Blues," and for the same reasons. As singer, Armstrong adopts the same suave manner as he did on trumpet, the same emphasis on graceful melodic cascades, rubato rhythms, portamenti, and triadic extensions. In the fifth measure he unveils the falling major seventh with an added thirteenth figure from "Savoy Blues," which he repeats in the minor mode in the next measure. The following two figures dwell on the major seventh, employing jagged intervals to create the same illusion of self-accompaniment heard in "Terrible Blues" (mm. 7–8). Finally, to open the last third of the progression (m. 9), Armstrong deploys an F minor seventh chord over a B♭⁷, savoring the "extended" harmonic effect thus produced, after which he oscillates between the tonic and the thirteenth (m. 10), again echoing "Savoy Blues."

EXAMPLE 6.3   Louis Armstrong and His Hot Five, "West End Blues," 28 June 1928, scat vocal-clarinet duet between Louis Armstrong and Jimmy Strong.

---

49 Hadlock, *Jazz Masters of the Twenties*, 38; Panassié, *Louis Armstrong*, 82.

In his piano solo on the fourth chorus, Earl Hines alternates between the two main topics of early jazz—sweet (or classical) for the first and last four measures (over striding accompaniment), and hot for the swinging double-time feel of the middle section. Finally, the last chorus juxtaposes the sweet against the gutbucket (example 6.1). Armstrong begins the chorus holding a high B♭ for four measures at a soft dynamic, echoing the opening of Bubber Miley's solo on Ellington's "Black and Tan Fantasy," recorded a year earlier. In the fifth measure Armstrong explodes into a series of descending blues phrases. Anchored to high B♭, Armstrong repeats five times a falling riff that emphasizes the minor seventh blue note—a classic blues phrase in the gutbucket tradition. After an intervening descent to the low register, Armstrong shifts gears and plays a sweeping scale to G, half-valves to high B♭, and falls back down to the major seventh of the chord, creating a glamorous mood far removed from the earnest blues figures only two measures earlier. Then the band stops and Hines plays in his words "a little bit of classic thing"—a falling series of crushed chords—before the horns return for the final cadence.[50]

Although gutbucket and sweet predominate in this chorus, other topics surface as well. Strikingly, the order of topics duplicates that of the first chorus, bringing the music full circle. Armstrong begins with the gutbucket approach; then in the seventh bar of the blues progression, just as in the first chorus, he inserts a brief passage in modified clarinet style; this yields, as before, to sweet style. And then, although Armstrong himself does not play in the next measures, pianist Earl Hines completes the pattern with classically oriented falling figures (mm. 67–69). Since the two choruses are not obviously linked by common motives (apart from the melody at the beginning of each), Armstrong would appear to be thinking purely in terms of a topical sequence to unite the beginning and ending of this remarkable recording.

THE AGE OF HYBRIDITY

All evidence suggests that Armstrong's recorded performance on "West End Blues" was carefully worked out in advance, though perhaps the component parts came together through several live performances over time. Zutty Singleton recalled the band rehearsing this tune in Lil's front room. Likewise, drummer George Wettling claimed to hear it at the Savoy

---

50 Collier, *Louis Armstrong*, 197.

Ballroom in a version that sounds similar to the recording: "When Louis started blowing the introduction to *West End Blues* (man, was it mellifluous), everybody in the ballroom started screaming and whistling, and then Louis lowered the boom and everybody got real groovy when he went into the first strains of *West End*."[51] It sounds like Armstrong used it as a set piece for his evening performances. In this sense he would have been following his own standard practice of refining his solos rather than creating them anew each time, a practice in evidence on "Cornet Chop Suey," "Big Butter and Egg Man," "S.O.L. Blues," and most of his solos with Fletcher Henderson. As he explained later in life, "And always, once you got a certain solo that fit in the tune, that's it, you keep it. Only vary it two or three notes every time you play it—specially if the record was a hit."[52]

During the first six months of 1928, unemployed (at first) and hounded by Reeves and Peyton, Armstrong would have had every incentive to plan performances that could cast him in the best possible light. Perhaps this incentive explains the lurch toward greater "sophistication" in the recordings from June and December. "West End Blues" outdoes all these in the conspicuousness of the high-class references. One can imagine Armstrong carefully working out the cadenza, assembling its discrete, preexisting components, and honing his etudelike ascent to high D with an eye toward keeping Reuben Reeves up at night. By the same token, none of Armstrong's other recordings take such pains to show a diversity of topics. In particular, his consistent progression from gutbucket to clarinet style to sweet to classical in the first and last choruses suggest a gamut-running thoroughness, as if Armstrong were auditioning for someone who wanted to know all the styles he had mastered. The full power of the recording, however, depends on a oneness of feeling, of character, of intent, that makes all the diverse elements seem natural and logical together. Armstrong always sounds like Armstrong, whether he adopts a sweet, hot, or classical manner. As beautiful as his opening classical arpeggios are on their own terms, one would never mistake the player for Herbert L. Clarke, just as one would never confuse his sweet interpolations with a passage from Guy Lombardo. Armstrong made all his materials his own. On "West End Blues," he even brought the rest of the band with him, aligning every-

51 Shapiro and Hentoff, *Hear Me Talkin' to Ya*, 118.
52 Quoted in Gushee, "Improvisation of Louis Armstrong," 313.

one in a unity of expression that is not always present in the early Hot Fives, when Armstrong sometimes appears to leave his bandmates far behind conceptually.

One suspects that it was partly this uncanny alchemy of style and thought that gave Armstrong an edge over Reeves and every other trumpet player of his generation. And while the polarity between sweet and hot was more widely recognized during the swing era, it is also true that the unexpected, overwhelming success of hot style was a triumph of hybridity. Duke Ellington, Benny Goodman, Count Basie, Tommy Dorsey—all found a rapprochement with sweet, classical, and other high-class stylistic markers that one would never have encountered in, say, the early recordings of King Oliver, a hot player of the old school. Armstrong was not the only pioneer for this sort of hybridity, but his preeminence made him an especially potent example. Notwithstanding his contributions in the areas of virtuosity, architectural coherence, harmonic improvisation, and high notes, without his consolidation of idioms in the late 1920s the evolution of jazz solo style as we know it might have taken a very different course.

EPILOGUE

No, I don't try to make an art of my music. Music is a day's work
and we all ought to do a day's work. That buys the pork chops.

— LOUIS ARMSTRONG

ONE OF THE BOOKS FOUND IN Louis Armstrong's personal library
after his death was J. A. Rogers's two-volume historical survey, *World's
Great Men of Color* (1947). An inscription by the author appears on the
inside front cover: "To Louis—who occupies a *very special pedestal* on
the *topmost* pinnacle in my esteem. May you find many pleasurable
reading hours in this book—and much to make you happy and proud
of your ancestry." Armstrong valued the gift enough to make a reading
list of important chapters, which he carefully identified by page number
and crossed out (or wrote "*finis*") as he completed. The list, organized
chronologically, included biographies of the following black luminar-
ies: Samuel Coleridge Taylor, Toussaint L'Ouverture, Frederick Douglass,
Paul Lawrence Dunbar, Bert Williams, Booker T. Washington, Marcus
Garvey, George Washington Carver, Jack Johnson, Roland Hayes, Paul
Robeson, Marion Anderson, Joe Louis, Thomas Bethune, R. Nathaniel
Dett, Joe Gans, Mary B. Talbert, A. Phillip Randolph, William Grant Still,

and Rudolph Dunbar. Notably, Armstrong's interests embraced not only musicians, entertainers, and prize fighters, but also writers and political leaders—a breadth which makes his final annotation all the more telling. At the end of the list Armstrong noted tersely: "S'All. No Du Boise," and helpfully added the page number of the chapter that was *not* to be read. Having already omitted from his list W. E. B. DuBois, the progressive intellectual giant of the early twentieth century, Armstrong wanted posterity to know that the omission was not an accident.[1]

Armstrong's hostility toward DuBois probably dates back to the 1920s. Although DuBois was "the widely-acknowledged 'leader of his people'" by this time, he was not well liked in the black community.[2] A Harvard PhD in history, DuBois advocated racial progress through education and political power, assets that seemed beyond the reach of most working-class blacks. DuBois envisioned a top-down advancement through the so-called Talented Tenth, an elite of black society who would take the steps necessary to achieve equality with whites. Culturally, he allied himself with the lofty goals and values of the Harlem Renaissance. He sought changes through the NAACP, a civil rights organization he had helped to found, and propounded his views from the editor's chair at *The Crisis*, the organization's official magazine. Neither the publication nor the organization enjoyed much popularity among the rank and file. Most working-class blacks "regard the NAACP as a Negro snob affair," a friend of DuBois wrote despairingly to him, "and I have been trying from Philadelphia to Topeka in the West to disabuse their minds of such a preposterous idea."[3] As for DuBois himself, he was aware that with the exception of a small group of ardent supporters, most African Americans viewed him with disinterest or active dislike. An editor of *The Negro World* boiled down DuBois's essential problem to one of arrogance. People felt "that the editor of *The Crisis* looked down upon the masses and their infirmities 'from the heights of his own greatness.'"[4]

How different DuBois appeared from his predecessor and political opponent, the outstanding black leader at the turn of the century, Booker T. Washington. Born into slavery, and educated at schools for freedmen after the Civil War, Washington made common cause with the common

---

1   Louis Armstrong Collection, Manuscripts, Box 3, Folder 2, Louis Armstrong Archives.
2   David Levering Lewis, *W.E.B. Du Bois: The Fight for Equality and the American Century, 1919–1963* (New York: Henry Holt, 2000): 21.
3   Lewis, *W.E.B. Du Bois*, 3.
4   Lewis, *W.E.B. Du Bois*, 230, 21.

folk. Fearing that direct confrontation with the white power structure would only backfire, he advocated incremental progress through self-improvement and temporary accommodation with the status quo. His was a bottom-up philosophy, stressing hard work, basic education, and a striving for financial freedom; high cultural achievements and political freedom could come later. "There is as much dignity in tilling a field as in writing a poem," he famously said.[5]

Washington's flinty determination and commonsense morality appealed to the vast majority of African Americans, most of whom held conservative political views. The *Chicago Defender* often expounded Washingtonian philosophy, even in the theatrical pages. Salem Tutt Whitney, an entertainment columnist, wrote articles on the virtues of responsibility, the evils of making excuses, and the power of self-determination. One column took a skeptical, satirical view of the New Negro: "Just as soon as I regain my one-time vigor…I am going to organize a one-man expedition to search for the 'New Negro' to which every Race pamphlet, newspaper and magazine makes such frequent reference….He must be a species of the genus homo."[6] Similarly, Dave Peyton published a multitude of Washingtonian homilies, urging musicians to pull themselves up by their bootstraps:

- Opportunity is all we want.
- Nothing comes to us easy. Hard work is the penalty we must pay for success.
- Make use of all idle time by learning some profession or trade; it may benefit you in years to come.
- Ability is what counts, and you can't take it away from a person.[7]

Modifying instructions on social etiquette frequently given to southern migrants upon their arrival in the North, Peyton gave his musician readers a list of "don'ts":

- Don't beat time with your feet.
- Don't smoke or drink on the band stand.
- Don't flirt with anyone in the audience.

---

5 Booker T. Washington, *Up from Slavery: An Autobiography* (New York: Doubleday, 1919), 220.

6 *Defender*, 11 December 1926, 7.

7 *Defender*, 9 January 1926, 6; 21 August 1926, 6; 5 December 1925, 6; 14 November 1925, 7.

- Don't cross your feet or legs when sitting in the orchestra.
- Don't knock other musicians or leaders.
- Don't pout on the stand.
- Don't loaf around pool halls and barber shops. Go home, get up early in the morning, and practice your instrument.

Finally, Peyton admonished musicians to think of their profession, hard-headedly, as a business, not an art. For him, commercialism was a good thing. To black players who knew some jazz tricks, he said, "Hold on to our stuff, boys, we can commercialize it just as the white brother is doing." To the socially careless or maladroit, he chided, "Let us make the public respect us and our profession. We should be regarded in communities just as the doctor, the lawyer, the business man, and people in other commercial walks of life."[8]

Armstrong, who lived much closer to the ground than Peyton did, seems to have absorbed Washington's ideals just as deeply as a young man. Like Washington, Armstrong was an accommodationist, determined to play—and win—by the rules of the white majority. In this endeavor he was largely successful, not only in his music but in his goals for racial advancement. After he had built his reputation through tireless labor, patiently working within the system over many years, Armstrong had his contracts stipulate, "I wouldn't *play* no place I couldn't *stay*." "I was the first Negro to crack them big white hotels," he said proudly. But he did not believe in activism. In 1957 he engaged in a rare act of protest, loudly canceling his Soviet tour for the U.S. State Department when Eisenhower hesitated to enforce desegregation in Little Rock. A decade later, however, he distanced himself from the civil rights movement, the legacy of DuBois. When asked about the subject during an interview in 1967, Armstrong seemed unimpressed with the political progress that had been made: "Passing all them laws to open everything up—fine, okay, lovely. But it ain't gonna change everybody's hearts....Naw, they can't undo all the years of damage by passing a few laws."[9] Armstrong seemed embittered by the racial turbulence of the 1960s, particularly the divisions and strife within the black community. In a scathing document from 1969 he accused young African Americans of laziness, jealousy, and—notably— pretentiousness with respect to education: "They would rather lazy away their time doing nothing. Or feel because they have diplomas...that the

<hr />

8   *Defender*, 27 February 1926, 6; 23 October 1926, 6; 3 July 1926, 6.
9   King, "Everybody's Louie," 66, 67.

world owes them something....Just a waste of money to some of the hep cats who graduated....I went only to fifth grade because I had to work along with my schooling....But we were happy."[10]

In Armstrong's moral universe, few shortcomings were more offensive than social or educational snobbery. We have already seen the friction caused by Lil Hardin's constant hectoring, an assault made sharper, no doubt, by her one-time enrollment at Fisk University. Even his beloved fourth wife, Lucille, irritated Armstrong with her highfalutin "sense of Aires."[11] Slights on the bandstand stung decades later. After leaving King Oliver in 1924, Armstrong applied for a job with society bandleader Sammy Stewart. "But I wasn't dicty enough, regardless of how good I played, I wasn't up to his society," he recalled bitterly in 1971.[12] Similarly, Armstrong faulted Fletcher Henderson for being "so carried away with that society shit and his education."[13] According to Jacob Stein, who spent an evening with him on one occasion, Armstrong loved to skewer affected speech: "If he said something a bit pretentious, he struck a pose of mock seriousness and then growled out deep-throated laughter."[14] Armstrong learned his contempt for snobbery from his mother, Mayann, a New Orleans domestic and part-time prostitute: "One thing, everybody from the church folks to the lowest gave her the greatest respect, and she was always glad to say hello to anybody, no matter who....And with it all, she held her head up at all times....I guess I inherited that part of my life from Mayann."[15] Given this egalitarian, nonjudgmental upbringing, it's no wonder Armstrong hated DuBois.

Armstrong's social and racial views cast light on his own opinion of the Hot Fives. Unlike critics, who revered these records as the first great works of art in jazz, Armstrong barely considered them. Certainly, at the time he made the records, they held little more than fleeting economic value for him. Later in life, he recalled, "when we made the Hot 5 and Hot 7 records, it was just pick up those cats and do it. And we didn't want no royalties, just pay me, man, give me that loot. Got $50 each for each session, just a gig to us and glad to do it so we could go up town and have a ball with the money."[16] Nor did his esteem for the Hot Fives increase

---

10 Armstrong, *Armstrong in His Own Words*, 10.
11 Armstrong, *Armstrong in His Own Words*, xviii.
12 Jones and Chilton, *Louis*, 235–36.
13 Quoted in Jones and Chilton, *Louis*, 237.
14 Jacob A. Stein, *Legal Spectator and More*, 3rd ed. (Washington, DC: TheCapitol.net, 2003), 188.
15 Giddins, *Satchmo*, 53.
16 Willems, *All of Me*, 31.

after their canonization by the critical establishment. In two volumes of recently published autobiographical writings, Armstrong fails even to mention them.[17] He discusses his tenures with King Oliver, Fletcher Henderson, Erskine Tate, and Carroll Dickerson. Why not the Hot Fives? In 1941 Armstrong made his perspective clear in a response to critic Leonard Feather's query about the most important events in jazz history:

> Well the first one was when Pops [i.e., Joe Glaser] booked me for my first commercial program over the—N.B.C.—for Fleischmann's Yeast[....] Then too—those pictures—"Pennies From Heaven"— "Artists 'N' Models"—"Everyday is a Holiday"—and that fine "Going Places".[18]

Armstrong was proudest of his public advances in the entertainment industry, especially when he broke color barriers in radio and film. Toward his more esoteric contributions to the language of jazz, he apparently remained indifferent or oblivious. In this sense, Armstrong followed a professional course advocated by Washington (and Peyton), a course targeting socioeconomic triumph rather than political power or artistic achievement. Elevating the Hot Fives as works of art would probably have struck Armstrong as "putting on airs."

This point helps explain the most controversial part of Armstrong's career: his embrace in the 1930s of entertainment values not always compatible with jazz as the critics defined it. Seeing this embrace as a betrayal of the musical ideals demonstrated in the Hot Fives, writers have interpreted his later music as a craven concession to the marketplace when other performers like Duke Ellington and Coleman Hawkins were staying true to their art. Thus, James Lincoln Collier speaks ominously of Armstrong's position in the early 1930s as a "fork in the road."[19] But from another perspective, Armstrong's road led in a remarkably straight line. As this book has tried to show, even his most innovative recordings in the Hot Five series stemmed somehow from economic exigencies of the moment, from prevailing novelty values, or possibly from his love of a

---

17 See Armstrong, *Louis Armstrong in His Own Words*; and Joshua Berrett, ed., *The Louis Armstrong Companion: Eight Decades of Commentary* (New York: Schirmer, 1999). Armstrong's treatment of the Hot Fives in "Jazz on a High Note" (1951) in *Louis Armstrong in His Own Words* came in response to a specific request from the editors of *Esquire*.

18 Armstrong, *Armstrong in His Own Words*, 147.

19 Collier, *Louis Armstrong*, 199.

particular sound. Most of all, the Hot Fives reflect Armstrong's desire to excel in his field—and not from any need to leave monuments for posterity. This same desire led him to perform on Broadway, to play hundreds of high Cs in Europe, to sing comedy songs, to play on the radio, and, finally, to appear in movies. Toward these goals, the Hot Fives served as mere stepping stones. Armstrong clearly regarded his engagements at the Vendome and the Savoy to be far more significant.

Armstrong's more holistic perspective can help shape our parting view of the Hot Five and Hot Seven recordings. Surely he is right that these records represented tiny blips on the crowded screen of his 1920s career. One can only imagine the exciting and innovative performances he played in live settings during this period. If oral histories are any indication, these events may well have eclipsed the most brilliant recorded solo we have, simply by virtue of their galvanizing public nature and sheer length (listeners report hearing twenty to thirty choruses at a stretch). Against this backdrop, I am reminded that my own lofty theories about his music are exercises in make-believe—plausible make-believe, I hope, but make-believe nonetheless. One night spent at the Savoy Ballroom in the summer of 1928, were such a journey possible, might call into question every idea in this book.

Yet even in light of clear limitations on the evidence of recordings, the Hot Fives have some advantages over the experience of hearing (or performing) the music in real time. As artificial as records may be, they do offer data points that can be charted in retrospect, and compared with relevant contemporaneous events, to perceive historical patterns of which even Armstrong himself might have been unaware. If we are chastened by a recognition of all that records leave out, we may nevertheless appreciate the powerful reflection they give of Armstrong's waking world in the 1920s. Coupled with newspaper reports and firsthand recollections, the Hot Fives may be brought to bear dynamic witness to the kind of player Armstrong was rapidly becoming within a changing environment. That, at least, has been the premise of this book.

And when all is said and done, of course, the Hot Fives are all we have to listen to. It is entirely just that we should prize them more than Armstrong did himself.

BIBLIOGRAPHY

ARCHIVES

Hogan Jazz Archive, Tulane University, New Orleans
Institute of Jazz Studies, Rutgers University, Newark
Louis Armstrong House and Archives, Queens College, New York

NEWSPAPERS

Chicago Defender
Chicago Savoyager
Chicago Sun-Times
Newsday
World Telegram and Sun Saturday Magazine
Zit's Theatrical Newspaper

BOOKS AND ARTICLES

Allen, Walter C. *Hendersonia: The Music of Fletcher Henderson and His Musicians.* Jazz Monographs, No. 4. Highland Park, NJ: author, 1973.

Allenbrook, Wye Jamison. *Rhythmic Gesture in Mozart: Le nozze di Figaro and Don Giovanni.* Chicago: University of Chicago Press, 1983.

Anderson, Gene. "The Origin of Armstrong's Hot Fives and Hot Sevens." *College Music Symposium* 43 (2003): 13–24.

Anderson, Gene H. *The Original Hot Five Recordings of Louis Armstrong.* CMS Sourcebooks in American Music, No. 3. Ed. Michael J. Budds. New York: Pendragon Press, 2007.

Armstrong, Lil Hardin. "Satchmo and Me." *American Music* 25 (2007): 106–24.

Armstrong, Louis. *Louis Armstrong in His Own Words: Selected Writings.* Ed. Thomas Brothers. New York: Oxford University Press, 1999.

———. *Satchmo: My Life in New Orleans*. New York: Prentice-Hall, 1954; reprint, New York: Da Capo, 1986.

Ayto, John. *Dictionary of Word Origins*. New York: Little, Brown, 1990.

Barker, Danny. *A Life in Jazz*. Ed. Alyn Shipton. London: Macmillan, 1986.

Barnhart, Robert K., ed. *The Barnhart Dictionary of Etymology*. New York: H.W. Wilson, 1988.

Bergreen, Laurence. *Louis Armstrong: An Extravagant Life*. New York: Broadway Books, 1997.

Berliner, Louise. *Texas Guinan: Queen of the Nightclubs*. Austin: University of Texas Press, 1993.

Berliner, Paul F. *Thinking in Jazz: The Infinite Art of Improvisation*. Chicago: University of Chicago Press, 1994.

Berrett, Joshua. "Louis Armstrong and Opera." *Musical Quarterly* 76, no. 2 (1992): 216–41.

———, ed. *The Louis Armstrong Companion: Eight Decades of Commentary*. New York: Schirmer, 1999.

Bigard, Barney. *With Louis and the Duke: The Autobiography of a Jazz Clarinetist*. Ed. Barry Martyn. London: Macmillan, 1985.

Black, Charles L., Jr. "My World with Louis Armstrong." *Yale Law Journal* 95 (1986): 1595–1600.

Bradley, Jack. "Trumpet Fanfare." *Saturday Review* (4 July 1970): 19, 51.

Bridges, Glenn D. *Pioneers in Brass*. Detroit: Sherwood Publications, 1965.

Brooks, Edward. *The Young Louis Armstrong on Records: A Critical Survey of the Early Recordings*. Lanham, MD: Scarecrow Press, 2002.

Brothers, Thomas. *Louis Armstrong's New Orleans*. New York: Norton, 2006.

Chapman, David L. *Sandow the Magnificent: Eugen Sandow and the Beginnings of Bodybuilding*. Urbana: University of Illinois Press, 2006.

Chilton, John. Liner notes to *Louis Armstrong, Volume IV: Louis Armstrong and Earl Hines*. Columbia Jazz Masterpieces, 1989.

Cline, Beverly Fink. *The Lombardo Story*. Don Mills, Ontario: Musson, 1979.

Collier, James Lincoln. *Louis Armstrong: An American Genius*. New York: Oxford University Press, 1983.

Condon, Eddie, and Richard Gehman, eds. *Eddie Condon's Treasury of Jazz*. New York: Dial Press, 1956.

Dance, Stanley. "Louis Armstrong, American Original." *Saturday Review* (4 July 1970): 13.

———. *The World of Earl Hines*. New York: Scribner's, 1977.

DeVeaux, Scott. *The Birth of Bebop: A Social and Musical History*. Berkeley: University of California Press, 1997.

Dodds, Baby, as told to Larry Gara. *The Baby Dodds Story*. Rev. ed. Baton Rouge: Louisiana State University Press, 1992.

Drew, Peter. "The Professional Viewpoint." *The Record Changer* (July–August 1950): 31, 46–47.

Driggs, Frank. "Don Redman: Jazz Composer-Arranger." *The Jazz Review* 2, no. 10 (1959): 6–12.

Dunner, Sherwin, and Richard Nevins, prods. *At the Jazz Band Ball: Early Hot Jazz, Song, and Dance*. 60 min., Yazoo Video, © 2000, videocassette.

Ellison, Ralph. *Shadow and Act*. New York: Random House, 1964.

Floyd, Samuel A., Jr. *The Power of Black Music: Interpreting Its History from Africa to the United States*. New York: Oxford University Press, 1995.

Freeman, Bud, in conversation with Irving Kolodin. "The Father and His Flock." *Saturday Review* (4 July 1970): 15–17.

Fucito, Salvatore, and Barnet J. Beyer. *Caruso and the Art of Singing*. New York: Frederick A. Stokes, 1922.

Gabbard, Krin. "Signifyin(g) the Phallus: Representations of the Jazz Trumpet." In *Jammin' at the Margins: Jazz and the American Cinema*, 138–59. Chicago: University of Chicago Press, 1996.

Garrett, Charles Hiroshi. *Struggling to Define a Nation: American Music and the Twentieth Century*. Berkeley: University of California Press, 2008.

Gates, Henry Louis, Jr. *The Signifying Monkey: A Theory of Afro-American Literary Criticism*. New York: Oxford University Press, 1988.

Giddins, Gary. *Satchmo*. New York: Doubleday, 1988.

Gilbert, Douglas. *American Vaudeville: Its Life and Times*. New York: Whittlesey House, 1940.

Givan, Benjamin. "Duets for One: Louis Armstrong's Vocal Recordings." *Musical Quarterly* 87 (2004): 188–218.

Gold, Robert S. *Jazz Talk*. Indianapolis: Bobbs-Merrill, 1975.

Grupp, M. "How Armstrong Hits the High Ones." *Metronome* (September 1938): 50, 55.

Gushee, Lawrence. "The Improvisation of Louis Armstrong." In *In the Course of Performance: Studies in the World of Musical Improvisation*. Ed. Bruno Nettl with Melinda Russell, 291–334. Chicago: University of Chicago Press, 1998.

———. *Pioneers of Jazz: The Story of the Creole Band*. New York: Oxford University Press, 2005.

Hadlock, Richard. *Jazz Masters of the Twenties*. New York: Macmillan, 1972; reprint, New York: Da Capo, 1988.

Harker, Brian. "Louis Armstrong and the Clarinet." *American Music* 21 (2003): 137–58.

———. "Louis Armstrong, Eccentric Dance, and the Evolution of Jazz on the Eve of Swing." *Journal of the American Musicological Society* 61 (2008): 67–121.

———. "'Telling a Story': Louis Armstrong and Coherence in Early Jazz." *Current Musicology* 63 (1999): 46–83.

Harker, Brian Cameron. "The Early Musical Development of Louis Armstrong, 1901–1928." PhD diss., Columbia University, 1997.

Herndon, Booton. *The Sweetest Music This Side of Heaven: The Guy Lombardo Story*. New York: McGraw-Hill, 1964.

Hersch, Charles. *Subversive Sounds: Race and the Birth of Jazz in New Orleans*. Chicago: University of Chicago Press, 2007.

Hitt, George L. "The Lead Trumpet in Jazz (1924–1970)." PhD diss., Indiana University, 1976.

Hodeir, André. *Jazz: Its Evolution and Essence*. Trans. David Noakes. New York: Grove Press, 1956.

Hodes, Art, and Chadwick Hansen, eds. *Selections from the Gutter: Jazz Portraits from "The Jazz Record."* Berkeley: University of California Press, 1977.

Iyer, Vijay. "Exploding the Narrative in Jazz Improvisation." In *Uptown Conversation: The New Jazz Studies.* Ed. Robert G. O'Meally, Brent Hayes Edwards, and Farah Jasmine Griffin, 393–403. New York: Columbia University Press, 2004.

Jackson, Preston. "Swinging Cats." *Jazz-hot* 3, no. 19 (1937): 5.

James, Harry. "Jammin with James." *Metronome* 54, no. 8 (1938): 13.

Jemie, Onwuchekwa, ed. *Yo' Mama! New Raps, Toasts, Dozens, Jokes & Children's Rhymes from Urban Black America.* Philadelphia: Temple University Press, 2003.

Jones, Max, and John Chilton. *Louis: The Louis Armstrong Story, 1900–1971.* London, 1971; reprint, New York: Da Capo, 1988.

Kahn, E. J. "Powder Your Face with Sunshine, Part 1." *The New Yorker* (5 January 1957): 48.

———. "Powder Your Face with Sunshine, Part 2." *The New Yorker* (5 January 1957): 35–57.

Kenney, William Howland. *Chicago Jazz: A Cultural History, 1904–1930.* New York: Oxford University Press, 1993.

King, Larry L. "Everybody's Louie." *Harper's Magazine* (November 1967): 61–69.

Kline, Beverly Fink. *The Lombardo Story.* Don Mills, Ontario: Musson, 1979.

Labov, William. *Language in the Inner City: Studies in the Black English Vernacular.* Philadelphia: University of Pennsylvania Press, 1972.

Lange, Arthur. *Arranging for the Modern Dance Orchestra.* New York: Arthur Lange, 1926.

Laurie, Joe, Jr. *Vaudeville: From the Honky-Tonks to the Palace.* New York: Henry Holt, 1953.

Leonard, Neil. *Jazz and the White Americans.* Chicago: University of Chicago Press, 1962.

Lewis, David Levering. *W.E.B. Du Bois: The Fight for Equality and the American Century, 1919–1963.* New York: Henry Holt, 2000.

Magee, Jeffrey. "'Everybody Step': Irving Berlin, Jazz, and Broadway in the 1920s." *Journal of the American Musicological Society* 59, no. 3 (2006): 697–732.

———. "The Music of Fletcher Henderson and His Orchestra in the 1920s." PhD diss., University of Michigan, 1992.

———. *The Uncrowned King of Swing: Fletcher Henderson and Big Band Jazz.* New York: Oxford University Press, 2005.

Maxile, Horace J., Jr. "Say What? Topics, Signs, and Signification in African American Music." PhD diss., Louisiana State University, 2001.

McCann, John Lawrence. "A History of Trumpet and Cornet Pedagogy in the United States, 1840–1942." PhD diss., Northwestern University, 1989.

Meckna, Michael. *Satchmo: The Louis Armstrong Encyclopedia.* Westport, CT: Greenwood, 2008.

Meryman, Richard. "An Authentic American Genius: An Interview with Louis Armstrong." *Life* (15 April 1966): 93–116.

Mezzrow, Milton "Mezz," and Bernard Wolfe. *Really the Blues.* New York: Random House, 1946; reprint, New York: Citadel Press, 1990.

Napolean, Art. "The Music Goes Down and Around." *Storyville* no. 37 (1 October 1971): 18–27.

———. "A Pioneer Looks Back: Sam Wooding 1967." *Storyville* 2, no. 9 (1967): 3–8, 37–39.

Owens, Thomas. "Charlie Parker: Techniques of Improvisation." PhD diss., University of California, Los Angeles, 1974.

Panassié, Hugues. *Louis Armstrong.* New York: Scribners, 1971; reprint, New York: Da Capo, 1980.

Panico, Louis. *The Novelty Cornetist*. Chicago: Forster Music, 1923.

Perretti, Burton. *The Creation of Jazz: Music, Race, and Culture in Urban America*. Urbana: University of Illinois Press, 1992.

Porter, Lewis. *Lester Young*, rev. ed. Ann Arbor: University of Michigan Press, 2005.

——. Liner notes to *Louis Armstrong and Sidney Bechet in New York, 1923–1925*. Smithsonian Recordings R026 (1981).

Porter, Lewis, and Michael Ullman, with Edward Hazell. *Jazz: From Its Origins to the Present*. Englewood Cliffs, NJ: Prentice Hall, 1993.

Raeburn, Bruce. "Louis and Women." Louis Armstrong Symposium, University of North Carolina–Chapel Hill, 2 March 2001.

Ramsey, Frederick, Jr., and Charles Edward Smith, eds. *Jazzmen*. New York: Harcourt Brace, 1939; reprint, New York: Limelight, 1985.

Ramsey, Guthrie P., Jr. *Race Music: Black Cultures from Bebop to Hip-Hop*. Berkeley: University of California Press; Chicago: Center for Black Music Research, 2003.

Ratner, Leonard G. *Classic Music: Expression, Form, and Style*. New York: Schirmer, 1980.

Richman, Saul. *Guy*. New York: RichGuy Publishing, 1978.

Rogers, J. A. "Jazz at Home." In *The New Negro: An Interpretation*. Ed. Alain Locke, 216–24. New York: Albert & Charles Boni, 1925; reprint, New York: Arne Press and the *New York Times*, 1968.

Russell, Bill. *New Orleans Style*. Comp. and ed. Barry Martyn and Mike Hazeldine. New Orleans: Jazzology Press, 1994.

S. D., Trav. *No Applause—Just Throw Money: The Book That Made Vaudeville Famous*. New York: Faber & Faber, 2005.

Schoebel, Elmer, and Herman Openneer Jr. "The Elmer Schoebel Story." *Doctor Jazz* 32 (October 1968): 6–7.

Schuller, Gunther. *Early Jazz: Its Roots and Musical Development*. New York: Oxford University Press, 1968.

——. *The Swing Era: The Development of Jazz, 1930–1945*. New York: Oxford University Press, 1989.

Semmes, Clovis E. *The Regal Theater and Black Culture*. New York: Palgrave Macmillan, 2006, 15.

Shapiro, Nat, and Nat Hentoff, eds. *Hear Me Talkin' to Ya: The Story of Jazz as Told by the Men Who Made It*. New York: Rinehart, 1955; reprint, New York: Dover, 1966.

Smith, Charles Edward. "The Making of a King." *The Record Changer* 9, nos. 6 and 7 (1950): 19–21, 45–46.

Snyder, Robert W. *The Voice of the City: Vaudeville and Popular Culture in New York*. New York: Oxford University Press, 1989.

Stearns, Marshall, and Jean Stearns. *Jazz Dance: The Story of American Vernacular Dance*. New York: Macmillan, 1968; reprint, New York: Da Capo, 1994.

Stein, Jacob A. *Legal Spectator and More*. 3rd ed. Washington, DC: TheCapitol.net, 2003.

Stewart, Rex. *Jazz Masters of the Thirties*. New York: Macmillan, 1972.

Sudhalter, Richard M., and Philip R. Evans. *Bix: Man and Legend*. New Rochelle, NY: Arlington House, 1974.

Taylor, Jeffrey. "Earl Hines and Black Jazz Piano in Chicago, 1923–28." PhD diss., University of Michigan, 1993.

Teachout, Terry. *Pops: A Life of Louis Armstrong*. Boston: Houghton Mifflin Harcourt, 2009.

Thieck, William A. *Thieck's Daily Studies for Cornet and Trumpet*. Milwaukee, WI: Herman Bechler, 1928.

Tucker, Mark. *Ellington: The Early Years*. Urbana: University of Illinois Press, 1991.

Wald, Elijah. "Louis Armstrong Loves Guy Lombardo! Acknowledging the Smoother Roots of Jazz." *Jazz Research Journal* 1 (2007): 129–45.

Wallace, Ed. "Dixieland's Satchmo." *World Telegram and Sun Saturday Magazine*, 31 October 1953 [1958?], 6.

Walser, Robert, ed. *Keeping Time: Readings in Jazz History*. New York: Oxford University Press, 1999.

Washington, Booker T. *Up from Slavery: An Autobiography*. New York: Doubleday, 1919.

Willems, Jos. *All of Me: The Complete Discography of Louis Armstrong*. Studies in Jazz, No. 51. Lanham, MD: Scarecrow Press, 2006.

Williams, Cootie. "Reminiscing with Cootie." Interview by Eric Townley. *Storyville* 71 (June–July 1977): 170–74.

Wright, Laurie. "Stella Oliver Talks." *Storyville* no. 141 (1 March 1990): 105–7.

Yanow, Scott. *Classic Jazz: The Musicians and Recordings That Shaped Jazz, 1895–1933*. San Francisco: Backbeat Books, 2001.

INDEX